Keeping Your Own Counsel

ASPEN SELECT SERIES

Keeping Your Own Counsel: Simple Strategies and Secrets for Success in Law School

Walter A. Effross
Professor of Law
American University Washington College of Law

Cover image credit: WR.LILI/stock.adobe.com

To contact Customer Service, e-mail customer.service@aspenpublishing.com, call 1-800-950-5259, or mail correspondence to:

Aspen Publishing
Attn: Order Department
PO Box 990
Frederick, MD 21705

Printed in the United States of America.

1 2 3 4 5 6 7 8 9 0

ISBN 978-1-5438-2833-7

About Aspen Publishing

Aspen Publishing is a leading provider of educational content and digital learning solutions to law schools in the U.S. and around the world. Aspen provides best-in-class solutions for legal education through authoritative textbooks, written by renowned authors, and breakthrough products such as Connected eBooks, Connected Quizzing, and PracticePerfect.

The Aspen Casebook Series (famously known among law faculty and students as the "red and black" casebooks) encompasses hundreds of highly regarded textbooks in more than eighty disciplines, from large enrollment courses, such as Torts and Contracts to emerging electives such as Sustainability and the Law of Policing. Study aids such as the *Examples & Explanations* and the *Emanuel Law Outlines* series, both highly popular collections, help law students master complex subject matter.

Major products, programs, and initiatives include:

- **Connected eBooks** are enhanced digital textbooks and study aids that come with a suite of online content and learning tools designed to maximize student success. Designed in collaboration with hundreds of faculty and students, the Connected eBook is a significant leap forward in the legal education learning tools available to students.

- **Connected Quizzing** is an easy-to-use formative assessment tool that tests law students' understanding and provides timely feedback to improve learning outcomes. Delivered through CasebookConnect.com, the learning platform already used by students to access their Aspen casebooks, Connected Quizzing is simple to implement and integrates seamlessly with law school course curricula.

- **PracticePerfect** is a visually engaging, interactive study aid to explain commonly encountered legal doctrines through easy-to-understand animated videos, illustrative examples, and numerous practice questions. Developed by a team of experts, PracticePerfect is the ideal study companion for today's law students.

- The **Aspen Learning Library** enables law schools to provide their students with access to the most popular study aids on the market across all of their courses. Available through an annual subscription, the online library consists of study aids in e-book, audio, and video formats with full text search, note-taking, and highlighting capabilities.

- Aspen's **Digital Bookshelf** is an institutional-level online education bookshelf, consolidating everything students and professors need to ensure success. This program ensures that every student has access to affordable course materials from day one.

- **Leading Edge** is a community centered on thinking differently about legal education and putting those thoughts into actionable strategies. At the core of the program is the Leading Edge Conference, an annual gathering of legal education thought leaders looking to pool ideas and identify promising directions of exploration.

In loving memory of

my mother, Dr. Susi Hillburn Effross,

and

my father, Dr. Harris I. Effross,

my first and best teachers;

and of

Professor Egon Guttman,

colleague, mentor, and—most of all—friend.

Contents

Preface (Or, the "Party" of the First Part)

In the late fall of 1984, towards the end of our first semester as Harvard Law School students, several classmates and I signed up to have lunch with one of our section's professors.

During that meal, he asked us, with what seemed to be genuine concern, whether we were feeling stressed, either in his course or generally. We all looked at each other; we all told him that we were just fine.

He was certainly too intelligent, and experienced, to believe us. Looking somewhat befuddled, he peered at us over his glasses and wondered, "Honestly, I don't know why you all don't treat law school as a three-year party."

My classmates and I looked at each other again. Somehow, we all managed to keep straight faces, but this time none of us had a ready answer for him.

Almost four decades—and numerous technological, cultural, political, social, and economic changes—after that lunch, it seems even less appropriate to compare law school to an extended party.

In fact, like the novel on which it was based (and like the television show which would follow in 1978), the 1973 movie *The Paper Chase* focused on the intense commitment, concentration, and hermetic (if not hermitic) existence of law students. Actor John Houseman's fictional Professor Kingsfield imperiously intoned, "You come in here with a skull full of mush, and you leave thinking like a lawyer."

Similarly intimidating is a book that a well-meaning relative gave me the summer before I started law school: *One L,* Scott Turow's account of his first-year experience at Harvard in 1975–76. (I found it so unnerving that I put it away after only a few chapters, and completed it ten months later, while returning home after final exams.)

During that summer, I scoured libraries and bookstores for any guide to this new environment, but came up with little that seemed useful, insightful, practical, or even particularly encouraging. (On an early visit to the campus, I'd asked an especially prominent professor, after one of his class sessions ended, whether he had any advice for a newly admitted law student: he'd answered, "I'm very tired now. Why don't you see me in the fall?")

The book that you are now reading contains my version of the information that I so nervously searched for in the spring and summer of 1984. It organizes and distills more than 25 years of advice that I've given to, and heard from, prospective students, students, and alumni as a member of the faculty of the

American University Washington College of Law (WCL); and, before that, as an adjunct faculty member at Seton Hall Law School.

These chapters also include lessons I that learned as a law student at Harvard, as a judicial clerk for the Supreme Court of New Jersey, and as an associate at two of New Jersey's largest law firms, Roseland's Lowenstein Sandler and Newark's McCarter & English. (There are no "composite characters," but in some cases personal details have been modified to protect the privacy of individuals.)

All the views expressed are my own and are not official statements or positions of any of these institutions. I have no financial interest in any of the books that I recommend, except for my own book on corporate governance; and I don't necessarily agree with every view expressed in them.

The material is arranged in roughly the order in which you might find it of use during your law school career. However, you might want to browse through the entire book before your first day of classes.

This is a book of "you might" and "you could," and even, "you should"; but never, "you must."

Rather than attempting to offer a complete, definitive, or one-size-fits-all guide to law school, *Keeping Your Own Counsel* suggests—and, in its eight appendices, provides further details and examples of—some simple and supportive strategies, systems, schedules, and structures, many of which you might not see or hear elsewhere, for engaging with and enriching your law school journey.

The title refers not only to the chapters' recommendations and reasons for constructing specific types of lists, but also to their emphasis on preparing a portable professional portfolio to maximize your career opportunities.

I hope that this book will help you navigate from acclimation to acclamation, and that it will make your law school experience, if not quite a three-year party, as productive, fulfilling, manageable, and meaningful—and as enjoyable—as it can be.

Walter A. Effross
January 2023

Acknowledgments

I thank Dean Roger Fairfax of the American University Washington College of Law (WCL) for his support of this project.

Earlier versions of elements of the following material appeared in supplements and handouts that I created for my WCL courses and presentations; in editions of my book, *Corporate Governance*; on my blog, GovernanceDrafting.com; and in my article, *Ten Tips for Landing J.D. Jobs for Law Students and Graduates*, in the *National Law Journal* on July 15, 2013.

Keeping Your Own Counsel

Chapter 1
Ten Principles of Success in Law School

First, it's certainly no surprise that in law school, "success," however you might define or measure it, depends on your ability to distinguish yourself from others applying for the same prizes, positions, or employment opportunities. Beyond your own classmates, approximately 40,000 students across the country will begin law school at the same time as you do.

However, **Remember that grades are an important way, but not the only way, to distinguish yourself.** Even single-minded studying won't necessarily guarantee good grades, because exams and the grading process aren't perfect or precise ways to measure your understanding of the material.

A few of my first-semester teachers tried to convince the class that "Grades don't matter," but I doubt that any of us ever believed that. However, as you progress in your career, your law school grades will become less important. Potential employers will probably be much more interested in the relevance to their work of your experiences in practice. In particular, law firms will consider how many current clients your expertise will be able to aid and how many new clients you can bring with you, or otherwise attract.

Second, **Learn the rules and guidelines**, not only those introduced at orientation and in your classrooms but also those that aren't necessarily written down.

Just as *The Paper Chase*'s James Hart wasn't aware that the reading assignment for his first class had been posted, many lawyers whose work regularly involves contacting their clients' creditors might have been surprised to discover that their activities are governed by the federal Fair Debt Collection Practices Act (1978), violations of which can make them liable for actual and punitive damages, and even subject them to disciplinary proceedings. More generally, a number of courts have developed their own procedural rules; in addition, less formal, but no less important, understandings underlie the widely varying "legal cultures" of different jurisdictions and/or fields of practice.

There are also "well-known" rules like *Robert's Rules of Order*, of which many people really only know the name, or perhaps just the rudiments. I advise my students to become familiar with and have handy a copy of the full and/or abbreviated versions of these rules, which might someday govern a meeting that they, a colleague, or a client is involved in or leading. (There are serious questions about the viability of these rules for board of directors' meetings and for shareholders' meetings; in fact, the American Bar Association has developed, and periodically revises, its own *Handbook for the Conduct of Shareholders' Meetings*.)

Third, **Don't live by default**, or by reaction. Instead, **Take the initiative and actively define (and, when necessary, redefine) your own personal focus**—to what ends you'd like to apply the skills and substantive knowledge that you're acquiring.

In this connection, you should **Stay alert to emerging issues**, particularly ones combining traditional practice areas and legal topics. Try to position yourself as someone who can not only summarize, explain, and help solve some of these problems but also anticipate new ones. To use two of the most beloved words of one dean I've worked with, you should always be "entrepreneurial" and ready to take advantage of "opportunities."

Some of those opportunities might not last very long. When I was in practice, I was invited on a number of occasions to review with partners and clients the intricacies of a new interpretation of the Bankruptcy Code that could seriously affect the structure of various transactions; a few years later, revisions to the Code eliminated that concern.

On the other hand, many legal issues that I began to work with in 1990, as a member of a firm's newly formed Computer & High Technology Law Group (which I privately considered the equivalent, for a lawyer, of being one of Marvel's five original X-Men), are still developing.

Your attentiveness will also help you notice what Andrew Grove, the former CEO and chairman of Intel Corporation, called "career inflection points" for your own professional trajectory. The final chapter of his classic book on business strategy, *Only the Paranoid Survive* (1996), explores this issue in depth and by itself is worth buying the book for. Grove's emphasis on responding to such changes quickly and decisively, while you still have viable options, was probably related at least in part to his experiences as a child and young man in Nazi-occupied Hungary and his emigration during the Hungarian Revolution of 1956 to Austria, and ultimately to the United States, which are discussed in his memoir, *Swimming Across* (2001).

Fourth, to help you find new issues, and to enrich, illustrate, and add perspective to the formal reading assignments for your classes, **Seek out supplemental materials**, many of which this book suggests. As an advertisement years ago for *Business Week* warned, "What you don't know can't help you."

In particular, **Don't overlook publicly available (and, often, free) materials.** Intelligence agencies carefully monitor such "open source" materials as mainstream media reports. And, in Edgar Allan Poe's 1844 short story, *The Purloined Letter*, police detectives famously failed to find the crucial document because the villain had been clever enough to have hidden it in plain sight.

This book highlights particular types of easily accessible information that can be surprisingly useful to law students and lawyers. Sometimes, as Yogi Berra said (and also used as the title of his memoirs), you can observe a lot by watching.

Fifth, **Promote yourself by building your professional portfolio and your network in tandem**, especially by writing articles and/or blogging. As discussed in detail in Chapter 18, as a law student you can start creating a powerful package of publications.

Your written work (and maybe even videos) will demonstrate that you focused on, and actively engaged with, particular issues (as opposed to your simply saying in an interview, "I think blockchain's very interesting"), and will also give potential employers a chance to evaluate your work for themselves (rather than relying just on your grades, or on recommendation letters). (My own introductory Web site on blockchain is blockchainforlawstudents.com.)

In addition, your writings will suggest to employers that you'll be able to effectively market yourself and your practice, which is increasingly a factor in law firms' partnership decisions. Finally, by contacting and asking for advice from practitioners and others during your writing process, you can establish professional relationships that might well reward you in many different ways.

Sixth, **Find your own style.** A few months before I joined the WCL faculty, a veteran law professor from another school promised to give me some teaching advice during an upcoming social event. Before he could get into any details that evening, he suddenly had to leave; but he put his hand on my shoulder and said, "Good teaching all comes down to: Be yourself in the classroom. You don't have to be Professor Kingsfield" of *The Paper Chase*.

Of course, you might sometimes be compelled to compromise. As a very junior associate, I once horrified a senior associate by submitting to her a draft letter that included the closing, "Sincerely." She insisted (for reasons that still evade me) that the only appropriate closing for such a professional communication was "Sincerely yours."

Seventh, **Trust your gut.** Although our profession emphasizes (and, some might say, weaponizes) verbal adeptness and rhetorical proficiency, don't downplay or disregard "bad vibes" that you get from some argument, person, organization, or situation, even if you can't identify precisely where that feeling came from. Listen to your intuitive, non-verbal "right brain," as well as your more rational, linear "left brain." (Whether and how you should, and whether you have a professional responsibility to, share such misgivings with your colleagues and/or client are interesting questions.)

Eighth, **Remember that you are unique, but not alone.** No one else will bring to the classroom your exact combination of talents, attributes, and perspectives. But if something's not clear to you—or if you disagree with an argument, position, perspective, or conclusion—you're almost certainly not the only person who has that reaction (or who doesn't necessarily want to say so in front of everyone else).

Near the end of my first semester as a law student, I organized and moderated a panel presentation on "Conquering the Stress of Law School Exams." It featured a yoga instructor, a psychologist on the law school's counseling staff, and one of our professors, and it was fairly well attended. A lesson I thought even more important than any of the information provided by the panelists was the number of classmates who, during the next week, privately and separately told me something like, "That program was a good idea. I would have gone, but I didn't want to be seen there."

You also don't have to feel alone in another way. Every law school offers, officially and unofficially, many different, and often-overlapping, communities to connect and belong to; and, as signs in many stores say, "If you don't see what you like, ask for it." Chapter 20 discusses the logistics of founding, or co-founding, new groups for students at your law school.

Ninth, **Beware of shortcuts**. The Talmud tells the story of a young man who advised, when giving directions to a traveler, "Sometimes the long way is the 'short way.'" Similarly, around 300 B.C.E., Euclid reportedly told the Egyptian ruler Ptolemy I that "There is no royal road to [learning] geometry."

There's no shortage of study aids for law students, including prepared "case briefs" outlining the court decisions in leading casebooks; commercial outlines of the materials presented in various courses; and other students' class notes from a previous semester of a course. However, at least at the beginning of your law school journey, you should take the time to master the skills of distilling caselaw and lecture notes into manageable summaries of your own.

You can compare your results with the versions included in the study aids (which might not always be correct or complete). In the same way, someone using a book of chess puzzles probably doesn't get anywhere close to internalizing the material, or to a true mental workout, if she keeps flipping to the answers without at least trying to work through the puzzles herself.

This book recommends that you **Work regularly and incrementally** (in the Italian expression, *Festina lente*, or Make haste slowly). As the title suggests, you should **Collect your thoughts**, literally, and yourself, figuratively, as you **Make and update lists and other compilations** of information. Those resources are not just effective tools for time management, but, properly used and regularly reviewed (for instance, to recognize patterns or trends), can help you maximize your law school experience and your short-term and even long-term opportunities for employment.

Tenth, **Aim for and appreciate, but don't overdo, simplicity**. In *Walden* (1854), Thoreau famously wrote, "Simplify, simplify, simplify!" Few remember, though, that in the book's first chapter he claimed to have discarded three pieces of limestone that he'd been keeping on his desk, once he realized that he'd have to dust them daily. (For that reason, paperweights bearing Thoreau quotations might be even more unintentionally ironic than the U.S. postage stamps issued in his honor in 1967 and 2017. In an essay nine years after the publication of *Walden*, Thoreau wrote, "In proportion as our inward life fails, we go more constantly and desperately to the post-office. You may depend on it, that the poor fellow who walks away with the greatest number of letters, proud of his extensive correspondence, has not heard from himself this long while.")

As Stewart Brand, the creator of *The Whole Earth Catalog* (1968), wrote in 1986 in his own journal, after considering the so-called "KISS" principle: "Keep it simple stupid, is a good way to keep it stupid."

However, consider also that the apparent simplicity of a legal article, book, or classroom lecture might, like Fred Astaire's grace in dancing with a hat rack in *Royal Wedding* (1951), belie an enormous amount of training, practice, and preparation "behind the scenes." As Ovid wrote, *"Ars est celare artem"*—"It is (true) art to conceal art." About two thousand years later, the character Abby Sciuto (Pauley Perrette), the original forensic lab wizard of television's *NCIS*, echoed to her crime-solving colleagues, "Just because I make it look easy, doesn't mean it is."

Inversely, the Socratic (and idiosyncratic) pedagogy of many law professors could be seen as deliberately creating complexity and confusion. In the classroom, the "short way" to deeper understanding might be the teacher's repeatedly modifying a question or the facts of a particular hypothetical situation, rather than immediately supplying a direct answer.

I discovered only while preparing for exams at the end of my first year that one of our professors had created on commercially available audiotapes a series of lectures that set out, very simply and clearly, the rules through which we'd just spent two semesters slogging Socratically, the "long way."

Chapter 2
Your Personal Purpose: Five Lists to Consider Creating

The first, simplest, and most important list that you might make, even before your first class begins, is also the most personal, and possibly the most private: Why are you going to law school? What skills do you want to gain? What substantive knowledge do you want to learn? And for what purpose(s)?

As you discover more practice areas, possibilities, and preferences, your answers will almost certainly change. But regularly revisiting, revising, and refining this list can give you additional grounding, clarity, and motivation. It could also help you, in the words of a bumper sticker that once I saw, "Remember Who You Wanted to Be."

Clarifying your purpose(s) will help you personalize your law school experience as you choose courses, identify and develop research and writing topics, and explore opportunities for professional networking and employment. In his chronicle of his student years at Harvard Business School, *Ahead of the Curve* (2008), Philip Delves Broughton repeated a possibly apocryphal story told to his class during orientation: A student, upset at not being accommodated by an administrator, finally said in frustration, "Why are you treating me like this? I'm the customer, goddamnit," only to be told, "No, you're not. You're the product." As "an informed customer" who "knows what she wants," you might find yourself better able to find or create options to serve your purposes.

In addition, whether or not you practice any form of meditation, for further focus you might at the beginning of your studying and class sessions adapt a purpose-based practice of some meditators: "setting an intention" that your efforts will be aimed towards a certain goal or goals.

Four other purpose-related lists that you might create during the course of your law school career are:

First, a list of the specific types of clients, constituents, or communities that you might like to help as a lawyer (or law student), whether full-time or on a pro bono (unpaid) basis.

- What causes resonate with you?
- What are their relative priorities to you?
- Would you want to, and can you think of ways to, serve several of those constituencies at the same time (including as pro bono projects while working at a law firm)?
- Are you interested in working as inside or outside counsel to a particular type of for-profit or nonprofit organization, in a particular industry or profession or with a particular method of operation?
- Might you want to someday start your own law firm, other business, or nonprofit entity for these purposes?
- Have you found any role models for the type of legal practice(s) in which you're most interested?

As early as during the summer before law school, you could check the Web sites of relevant organizations, and even contact them, to see what legal issues they're currently concerned with. You might also contact faculty at your law school who work or have worked on those issues or with those groups.

Saving, whether digitally or in hard copy, some of the material from those sites—and including the dates that you collected it—could give you a useful perspective on their content months (or years) later.

For general background and perspectives on a range of issues, you could visit the Web sites of (and possibly join) the American Constitution Society (acslaw.org; progressive) and/or The Federalist Society (fedsoc.org; conservative).

Second, you might compile a list of demographic, cultural, environmental, and technological changes that you believe are, or will become, particularly relevant to the groups, businesses, and organizations of interest to you, especially if you see them as creating new areas of practice. They could, for instance, combine existing concerns in new ways: For example, What are the tax and other legal considerations of participants when a nonprofit organization raises funds by auctioning off NFTs that it's created (or had third parties create) from content donated to it for that purpose by celebrities?

Among the aphorisms posted on his blog and collected in his book, *Excellent Advice for Living* (2002), Kevin Kelly, the founding executive editor of *Wired* magazine, observed that, "The greatest rewards come from working on something that nobody has a name for. If you possibly can, work where there are no words for what you do."

Third, even if only for yourself, you might formulate what has sometimes been called an "elevator speech" or "elevator pitch"—a brief statement of your purpose or focus, as if you had only the few moments during an elevator ride to describe these to a potential employer or investor.

Although they might not exactly fit that description, I've been impressed by the powerful simplicity of two examples: "Help Right Wrongs," which my father often told me was featured, decades ago, in the ACLU's ads in New York's subway cars; and a message that I recently saw on a signboard outside a Maryland church, "Find Hope Here."

Fourth, make a list of themes of your different activities and interests to date. As Kierkegaard wrote, "Life must be understood backwards, but lived forwards."

I once attended, with dozens of other new law professors, a several-day program that offered advice on developing and balancing our teaching, scholarship, and service. One of the highlights was a lengthy presentation by a highly regarded senior academic who encouraged each of us to find one big idea to work on throughout our entire academic careers.

At the time, that advice struck me as extremely impractical. Even if someone could identify and start writing about an extraordinary idea, how could she prevent others from addressing it themselves?

Today, I disagree even more strongly with that approach. However, I've noticed that, although I didn't always emphasize all of them or their interconnections at the time, particular themes have wound through some of my own work over the years.

Making, reviewing, and updating this list during and after your law school experience could help you appreciate the ways in which lawyers are able to (like Madonna, in her own profession) repeatedly reinvent aspects of their work, and reposition themselves, over the course of their careers, particularly as new areas of legal practice emerge.

(For this reason, you might also save a copy of the course list for your final year of law school—years later, you might be surprised to see which areas were just beginning to be, or weren't, addressed.)

Chapter 3
Five (and Ten More) Reading Suggestions for Your Pre-1L Summer

What should you read during the summer before you start law school?

For previous generations, popular recommendations included: Karl Llewellyn's *The Bramble Bush: On the Law and Its Study* (1933); Justice Benjamin Cardozo's *The Nature of the Judicial Process* (1921); and Justice Oliver Wendell Holmes Jr.'s *The Common Law* (1881).

My own suggestions (in order of priority, but I most strongly recommend the first five items) are:

First, check your law school's Web site for the rules of conduct governing law students (some of which may apply to all students, and/or all members, of the university's community). Particularly note the provisions of the honor code, especially any definitions of plagiarism (which is an academic, not necessarily an intellectual property law, offense); and, any policies concerning or regulating speech and conduct (inside and outside the classroom, and online). (Of course, law schools that are part of state universities rather than of private institutions will also be governed by the First Amendment.)

Second, browse through the "Obama Administration Questionnaire" (available online), a seven-page list of 63 questions circulated by President Barack Obama's staff in November 2008 for those interested in applying for positions with his incoming administration. At the time, some commentators speculated that the questionnaire's depth and comprehensiveness would discourage many qualified candidates from applying. Consider that you might be required to answer, in years to come, some of these (or similar) questions, especially if you apply for a sensitive position with a government agency, or for a judicial position.

Third, skim the agency section of the current edition (fifth, as of this writing) of Daniel Kleinberger's *Examples and Explanations: Agency, Partnership & LLC Law*.

Although agency law probably won't be among your required first-year courses, it would be a very practical subject for a "bridge," "commons," or similar set of sessions that bring together the teachers of your separate classes to discuss a common theme. The field unites aspects of torts, contracts, and criminal law in examining, among other issues, the ways in which one person or company can be considered an "agent" for a second party (the "principal"); and how an agent's (or a self-professed agent's) interactions with a third party could make the agent and/or the principal (or purported principal) liable to that third party, even if the agent's actions were mistaken, misinformed, negligent, or criminal.

Fourth, skim online the American Bar Association's Model Rules of Professional Conduct (themselves special applications of agency law, where lawyers and law firms act as agents for one or more clients, their principals), including the official comments. The rules themselves are fairly straightforward, if (necessarily) imprecisely phrased, and provide a useful overview of the sometimes-conflicting responsibilities of all lawyers not just to all of their clients but also to the court system. You'll probably be required to take a course in Professional Responsibility, and the MPRE (Multistate Professional Responsibility Examination), during your second or third year.

Fifth, check out the American Bar Association's Web site (americanbar.org), which features dozens of member groups, to get a sense of the types of possible areas of practice and of the issues that are arising in each. As a law student, you'll be eligible to join the ABA, and to attend the meetings and receive the publications of its sections, for free or for a nominal price.

Sixth, many useful lessons applicable to the work of lawyers can be drawn from David Priess's book, *The President's Book of Secrets: The Untold Story of Intelligence Briefings to American Presidents from Kennedy to Obama* (2016), which provides an in-depth discussion of the ways in which advisers (in this case, intelligence agencies, particularly the CIA) prepare manageable summaries of extremely complex issues for extraordinarily busy "clients" or "principals," and how they adapt their written and oral briefings to the styles of different administrations. (For a deeper discussion of this topic, see Appendix A, *Thirteen Aspects of Preparing and Presenting "Actionable" Advice*.)

Seventh, if you'd like an advance look at the material for any of your first-semester courses, you might skim the corresponding books in the "Examples and Explanations" series. A more stripped-down, nuts-and-bolts overview of some of this material would also be available in a "multistate" study guide from one of the leading bar review courses.

Eighth, Nobel Prize-winner Daniel Kahneman's *Thinking, Fast and Slow* (2011) presents a sobering survey, by a pioneer of "behavioral economics," of the varieties of cognitive traps that can plague casual, and even careful, decision makers—including counsel, clients, and judges. (See also Appendix B, *Enhancing the Decision-Making Process*.) Another useful approach to decision-making, not only routinely but in crisis situations, is Atul Gawande's *The Checklist Manifesto: How to Get Things* Right (2009), in which a surgeon and medical school professor reviews the role and limitations of checklists in the medical context and beyond.

Ninth and Tenth, I highly recommend two complementary approaches to productivity. David Allen's classic *Getting Things Done: The Art of Stress-Free Productivity* (2001) sets out a system for organizing all sorts of information, based on the practice of writing down ideas and information rather than trying to keep them all in your memory. By contrast, Oliver Burkeman's *Four Thousand Weeks: Time Management for Mortals* (2021) stresses the overarching importance of clarifying one's goals and priorities rather than continually searching for new productivity techniques in an attempt to accomplish everything.

Eleventh, if you haven't already encountered them, browse through a few of the *Dialogues* of Plato (such as *Protagoras*, *Gorgias*, *Meno*, and *Phaedrus*), which present Socrates' rhetorical tactics for exposing the mistakes, misconceptions, and misunderstandings of his associates. (His famously deceptive claims of ignorance gave rise to the term, "Socratic irony.") The "Socratic method" of classroom discussion—notably featured in the novel, movie, and television show, *The Paper Chase*—remains an integral part of many law school courses, particularly during the first year.

Twelfth, browse through a book-length biography of a judge. What does it say about her path to, and through, law school? How did her personal and professional experiences before being elevated to the bench shape her judicial philosophy? How, if at all, did that philosophy change over her time on the bench? What part did she play in the decisions and dynamics of the court(s) of which she was a member?

Thirteenth, skim a copy of mythologist Joseph Campbell's 1949 classic, *The Hero with a Thousand Faces*, or read online summaries of his "monomyth," a universal narrative structure in which a protagonist leaves his or her home, engages in adventures, and returns to the community with new powers and abilities. In this sense, you and your classmates could all be considered heroes. Notable responses and reactions to Campbell's work include Maria Tatar's *The Heroine with 1001 Faces* (2021) and Christopher Vogler's *The Writer's Journey: Mythic Structure for Storytellers & Screenwriters* (1992, but also in several subsequent editions).

Fourteenth, for contrast with your own journey, and to better understand the professional training of potential future clients, you might be interested in accounts of the business school experience—which, for instance, emphasize the importance, and even requirement, of students' working in groups. The most recent book of this type might be Philip Delves Broughton's *Ahead of the Curve: Two Years at Harvard Business School* (2008). Earlier portrayals include Peter

Robinson's *Snapshots from Hell: The Making of an MBA* (1994, about Stanford Business School); Robert Reid's *Year One: An Intimate Look Inside Harvard Business School* (1995); and Peter Cohen's *The Gospel According to the Harvard Business School* (1973).

Fifteenth, when you know the names of the faculty teaching your first semester's courses, check their pages on the law school's Web site. You might consider browsing through some of their most recent work if it's easily available online. You could also e-mail one or more of them to introduce yourself and ask for their suggestions for reading (for the course, or for law school preparation in general).

Over the summer, you might ask your undergraduate college or university's career services and/or alumni offices for the names of alumni who practice in legal fields, in geographical areas, and/or with employers of interest to you, especially if those alumni also attended your law school. Some of those alumni could suggest material to read and other people to contact, and might answer what could be the most valuable general question of all: "Is there anything else that you think I should know [or, that I should keep in mind]?"

Chapter 4
Nine Differences Between College and Law School

First, unlike college, in your first year you'll be assigned to most if not all of your courses (typically including Contracts, Torts, Civil Procedure, Property, and Criminal Law).

Second, you'll usually be taking those courses with the same subgroup (often a quarter or fifth) of your entering class.

Some sessions, like those on legal writing, could divide your "section" of the class into even smaller groups. Before you get a chance to select courses for your second and third years, you'll have been immersed in, and involved in forming, the culture and community of your section, which might differ significantly from those of other sections.

Third, because law schools generally don't have "majors" as such, you're more free to pursue (or design) your own, and your own degree of, specialization when choosing upper-level courses, and possibly internships or externships.

Fourth, despite the different areas of law and different types of employers that you and your classmates will be choosing among (for instance, large law firms, small firms, state or federal agencies, advocacy or other nonprofit groups, in-house positions, or solo practice), the shared experience of law school will probably give you more in common academically with (and more post-graduation opportunities to interact professionally with) your law school classmates than with your college classmates.

Fifth, unlike many of your college courses (such as those focusing on ancient history or on classic works of literature), most of your law school courses should recognize that during the course of your career, and even during the remainder of your time at law school, some of their substance will change, often significantly, as the result of new technologies, emerging or re-invigorated intellectual theories, and shifting cultural emphases and priorities. As a lawyer, and maybe even as a law student, you might be able to contribute to and influence some of those changes.

Sixth, unlike your freshman year courses in college, your first-year law school courses, and many of those in your second and third years, will probably involve the same general teaching methods, materials, and forms of final exams. (Chapters 13, 15, 16, and 22 discuss preparation for and participation in class, constructing course outlines, preparing for exams, and taking exams.)

Seventh, many of your law school courses might not have a midterm. During my first year, one of the full-year courses for my section had only one exam, at the end of the academic year. In any of those situations, it's tempting but dangerous to postpone exam review until close to exam period, especially because it can be easy to lose track of how much material the class has actually covered.

Eighth, you might well find fewer (but might consider creating) extracurricular groups, whether officially recognized or more informal, that are organized just for fun, as opposed to those involving some form of the study, practice, or discussion of law. Chapter 20 reviews some aspects of founding or co-founding a student group.

Ninth, even as a law student you might find non-lawyers intimidated by your presence (particularly if you start asking questions and taking notes, even if you're simply writing down the names of participants and a chronology or timeline of events). For instance, a number of law students have told me they believed that after health care providers asked their occupation, they or their relatives immediately seemed to receive more attentive care.

Chapter 5
Fourteen Ways Law School Might Affect Your Thinking

Although the stereotype of a prospective law student is "someone who really likes to argue," going to law school might not make someone even more disputatious.

Instead, it might be more accurate to say that law school helps students reason and argue more effectively and sensitizes them to linguistic ambiguity and to issues of potential liability.

Carl Sagan, the astronomer, astrophysicist, and popularizer of science who was most well-known for hosting the 1980s PBS television series, *Cosmos*, observed that "Science is much more than a body of knowledge. It's a way of thinking." The same could be said of each course in the law school curriculum, considered deeply enough, and for the collection of courses completed by any law student before graduation.

Among the ways in which you might find your thinking changing during law school are:

First, law students are trained to question not only assumptions, but also definitions. For instance, how does one define the "fair" price of an item, or when someone has made a "reasonable" effort to fulfill her part of an agreement? One of my classmates, who had majored in science, said that as we began our first year, he "went from answering questions to asking them."

One of the first panel presentation programs that I organized as a law professor was "Close Encounters with the Fourth Estate: Responding to and Contacting the Media." I was surprised to learn that there was no precise definition of an "off the record" or "deep background" conversation, and that a careful lawyer or client should make sure that she and the journalist (whom of course she would ultimately have to trust) agreed in advance on how information furnished during particular interactions could, or could not, be used and attributed.

Similarly, among law firms, the status and authority of a lawyer with a position identified as "counsel," or "of counsel," can vary widely (possible meanings include: a semi-retired partner; someone being considered for partnership; and, a law professor or other outside legal expert affiliated with the firm for certain projects).

In the law-firm context, even the term "partner" is ambiguous. For the last several decades, law firms have used the word in both internal and public communications to refer not only to a traditional "equity partner" who holds a significant share of the firm's profits and has a substantial voice in its management but also to a "non-equity partner" (sometimes known as a "salary partner") who meets neither of these criteria.

Second, law students should become less likely than the general public to be impressed or intimidated by someone's credentials and supposed expertise, and more interested in determining her familiarity with the facts of the situation at issue and exactly how she used those facts to reach her conclusions. The Evidence course involves, among other topics, how a lawyer can establish (or challenge) an individual's qualifications and conclusions as an "expert" in a particular field.

Third, law students will appreciate that providing appropriate advice to a client involves the facts of his specific situation. As an illustration "close to home," it might not help a law student as much as she might expect to ask a substantive question of someone who teaches or is a classmate in another section of one of her courses: The most "correct" answer might depend in part on the context in which the material was presented in her own class. In practice, I quickly learned to ask, if it hadn't been stated when I was given a research assignment, the specific federal and/or state jurisdictions that I should focus on.

Fourth, law students may become more interested in verifying information for themselves (especially by using primary sources), after having become more keenly aware of the perils of misprints, misquotations, misinterpretations, inexpert paraphrasing, and reading quotations out of context. They might also be more inclined to challenge statistical arguments and to question the ways in which the data were collected and analyzed. (See, for instance, the conclusion of Chapter 19.)

Fifth, law students will become more attuned to the necessity of clear communication, to prevent even unintentional misperceptions, misunderstandings, and misrepresentations—by themselves, their clients, courts, and the general public. For instance, many contracts introduce with the phrase, "For the avoidance of doubt," what could be seen as a normally unnecessary clarification of a term or other element. Lawyers might also specify processes for the parties' transmission, and for the verification of their receipt (and even of the content), of communications.

In a musical analogy that might be called the Springsteen Syndrome, law students should be listening carefully to a song's words, especially when they seem to be at odds with the tone and mood of the music. In 1984, the songwriter and musician was reported to be unhappy with the use by Ronald Reagan's presidential campaign of the newly released album's title track, *Born in the U.S.A.*, whose tragic lyrics undercut the pulsing power of the music and its apparently patriotic refrain. (By some accounts, Springsteen began performing the song solo, on acoustic guitar, so that his audience could more fully appreciate the words.)

Moreover, some have suggested that the title of Springsteen's propulsive *We Take Care of Our Own* (2012), which was used by Barack Obama's reelection campaign (and played at the presidential victory speeches of Obama and of Joe Biden) was, in light of that song's lyrics, intended as ironic. Finally, the upbeat rhythm of *Glory Days* (1984) masks its protagonists' wistful reflections that their high school years were the high points of their lives.

Sixth, law students, and lawyers, could find themselves interpreting questions or statements more literally than had been intended. In his memoirs, *Company Man* (2014), John Rizzo recalled that when he was general counsel for the CIA, "a very promising young attorney" (who was ultimately hired) had difficulty passing the standard polygraph examination. Rizzo was told that, when asked to confirm his place of birth, the lawyer had responded that "he can't be sure because he doesn't remember being there at the time." (Lawyers in particular might be reluctant to attempt sarcasm or humor online if their remarks could be taken literally.) Because of the many creative but justifiable ways in which law students can interpret multiple-choice questions and their possible answers, I don't use that form of question on my final exams.

Seventh, their training in "issue-spotting," as tested by the hypothetical situations appearing on law school exams, could lead students to emphasize potential problems with clients' proposed actions or arrangements. Unless their lawyers also suggest constructive solutions to these concerns, many clients (or potential clients) will stereotype counsel as "deal-killers," and consult them, if at all, too late in the deal-making process to receive the most effective and timely legal advice.

Eighth, law students will probably become even more interested in reducing arrangements to writing (and not necessarily to a simple or short document), even though in some situations this attempt might undermine or actually destroy the parties' relationship. For instance, it might not be wise, from a personal if not necessarily a legal standpoint, to ask one's romantic partner to sign a nondisclosure agreement before sharing a business idea with him or her.

On a corporate level, Mark Benioff, the founder, chairman, and CEO of Salesforce, promoted in *Behind the Cloud* (2009) his company's tendency to use, particularly "in international situations where we don't want to appear to be litigious Americans and we want to build a strong relationship with the partner or vendor," "[a] well-drafted contract with 'light and love'," that is, "a one-page document that is bulletproof and executed perfectly — with as little legal language as possible. . . The key is that it is tight enough to be binding, but loose enough to give latitude so that each party can operate freely. . . ."

Ninth, law students will be listening for what a statement, court decision, news report, or other document does *not* say. In Arthur Conan Doyle's 1892 short story, *The Adventure of the Silver Blaze*, Sherlock Holmes solved a crime by focusing on "the curious incident of the dog in the night-time." When one of his companions observed, "The dog did nothing in the night-time," Holmes responded, "That was the curious incident," and concluded that the perpetrator must have been someone familiar to the dog, who otherwise would have barked.

When I was in practice, I spent parts of many evenings and weekends writing articles for the *New Jersey Law Journal* and other publications about new decisions in bankruptcy law and in (what was then known as) "computer law." One of the most interesting but time-consuming aspects of analyzing the decisions was identifying their practical implications for clients. When I heard other lawyers summarize those decisions for each other, I sometimes noticed that they focused mostly on what the courts had explicitly stated; I wondered whether they hadn't explored some of the deeper areas, or just didn't feel like sharing their conclusions.

Tenth, after studying in detail numerous court decisions generated by the disintegration of commercial and/or personal relationships, law students might be somewhat less optimistic about the long-term prospects of any such arrangements. Whether or not law students as a group tend to be risk-averse, their legal education could well instill some "professional pessimism."

Eleventh, law students might fall into the trap of resolving complex and technical legal issues while losing sight of their larger context. For instance, however careful a lawyer is in drafting a contract or complaint, the other party still might not have the money or other means to satisfy its legal obligations to his client.

On a much more disturbing level, Richard Weisberg's *Poethics and Other Strategies of Law and Literature* (1992) includes an extended discussion of, and photographic reproductions of documents in which, lawyers in Vichy France (1940-1944) parsed the fine points of rules for identifying individuals as Jewish, without necessarily contemplating the inhuman applications of their dispassionate analyses.

Twelfth and Thirteenth, as a result of many of the above factors, law students may become reconciled to the inevitability of at least some level of ambiguity and inaccuracy; but they might also become abidingly suspicious of both supposedly simple questions and seemingly certain answers.

(Fourteenth, some might find themselves more inclined to construct numbered lists.)

Chapter 6
Thirteen Themes: A Starter Set

In 1952, the *Encyclopaedia Britannica* included, as part of its fifty-four-volume *The Great Books of the Western World* collection, the two-volume work *A Syntopicon: An Index to the Great Ideas*, which discussed 102 concepts (ranging from "Angel" to "World") that connected those books.

Since its first publication in 1976, the quarterly magazine *Parabola: The Search for Meaning* (parabola.org) has devoted each issue to a different spiritual theme, from "Ancestors" to "Ways of Knowing."

You might consider, through your law school career, what themes underlie courses across the curriculum. Among them could well be the following:

First, **Decision-making**. The majority of your reading assignments, at least during your first year, will consist of judicial decisions, and, one way or another, classroom discussion will focus on how to present arguments that persuade judges to rule for your clients.

On another, perhaps less-discussed, level, legal training also addresses how a lawyer can help clients to reach their own decisions beyond providing specific legal recommendations—how to be a true counselor, rather than simply a legal technician. That might involve a holistic approach, such as asking a client to consider whether, even if a court might ultimately find in his favor as a matter of law, protracted litigation would be in the best interests of his health.

A lawyer might also assist clients, particularly companies and other organizations, in designing, clarifying, and implementing their own decision-making processes and procedures.

In his extraordinary and humbling book, *Thinking, Fast and Slow* (2013), Nobel Prize-winning economist Daniel Kahneman, a pioneer of behavioral economics, concluded that, "Organizations are better than individuals when it comes to avoiding errors, because they naturally think more slowly and have the power to impose orderly procedures. Organizations can institute and enforce the application of useful checklists, as well as more elaborate exercises."

Appendix B, *Enhancing the Decision-Making Process*, describes many of the cognitive pitfalls carefully catalogued by Kahneman and other experts, and recommends that lawyers consider not only how they can avoid these traps but how they can help their clients install systems to decrease the clients' vulnerabilities. (It is also possible, if not necessarily ethical, to read such materials as manuals of methods by which to exploit others.)

Second, **Rules of and methods for interpretation**—of statutes, regulations, and agreements.

For example, there have been dozens of law review articles (one of them mine) about the Supreme Court's approach to interpreting the Bankruptcy Code, and in particular about Justice Scalia's insistence on embracing what he seemingly had no trouble identifying as (although Circuit Courts of Appeals had sometimes failed to agree on) the "plain meaning" of the relevant provisions.

- When, and in what order, should courts look to such sources as: a statute's legislative history, the larger historical context of its drafters, and various dictionaries' definitions of particular words or terms?
- In resolving ambiguities in a contract, when and how should courts consider the ways in which particular professions, industries, cultures, or communities use those words or terms, and the ways in which the parties involved in the specific situation at issue used those words or terms in their earlier dealings with each other?

Third, the crucial role of lawyers in identifying, estimating, and **Reducing risks in clients' relationships** with other parties—often by clarifying and specifying the parties' expectations—while recognizing that not every client will have the same appetite for, or tolerance of, risk.

A related theme is that of **Encouraging responsible risk-taking**: for instance, the "business judgment rule" puts the burden on shareholders to show that an executive's or board's costly mistake was the result of carelessness or disloyalty before the court will impose personal liability on those individuals. In Ken Burns' PBS television series, *Jazz* (2001), the prominent clarinetist and Big Band leader Artie Shaw criticized a leading competitor: "Glen Miller's band never ever made a mistake. And if you don't make a mistake, it shows you're not trying: you're playing within limits." Similarly, in a 2002 meeting that gave a title to a 2018 book about the criminal (un)accountability of executives, James Comey, as the incoming U.S. Attorney for the Southern District of New York, asked his criminal prosecutors which of them had never had an acquittal or a hung jury, and then unexpectedly derided that group as "the Chickenshit Club," for prioritizing win-loss records over the interests of justice.

Fourth, the role of **Defaults** and the ways in which to draft around them (for instance, by including disclaimers in a contract).

Starbucks aficionados know that they can order a "short" cup of hot coffee (8 liquid ounces, rather than the 12 in a "tall" cup) or a "trenta" cup of iced coffee (30 ounces, rather than 20 in the "venti" cup), even if those sizes aren't listed on the menus posted in the store. Similarly, what choices does a client have under a contract or the law, even if they aren't specifically identified? Some "enabling" statutes, like the Delaware General Corporation Law (DGCL), not only specify various legal options but also indicate that some of their lists aren't exclusive or exhaustive; that is, that there are valid possibilities that are not explicitly stated.

On the other hand, are there some guardrails or baselines that even sophisticated clients should not be able, as a matter of state and/or federal law, to contract around by their own "private ordering" of rights and responsibilities?

Fifth, the existence and effect of **Markets**, not just for individual lawyers and law firms but for the laws themselves.

For example, corporations can generally choose, wherever their operations are physically based, to incorporate themselves in any one of the states. Much has been written about the history of, and reasons for, Delaware's extraordinary dominance of the "market" for such incorporations, and about whether that state's overwhelming popularity represents a "race to the top" or a "race to the bottom" among competing states (and their respective corporate statutes). Commentators have also addressed at length the apparent competition among various federal jurisdictions (led by the District of Delaware, and the Southern District of New York) for the bankruptcy filings of major companies, which often have (or can create for themselves) several jurisdictional options in such a situation.

Sixth, as noted in Chapter 5, the necessity of **Clear communication**. During my first-year class in Property, I lost track of how many times our professor, a leading light of the Critical Legal Studies movement, referred to the law's "gaps, conflicts, and ambiguities." (Traditionally, each section ordered a T-shirt with its seating chart on the back and a classroom quotation from one of its teachers on the front: We chose his, "This is how lawyers numb their minds: with the narcotic of meaningless rhetoric.")

How could statutes, regulations, contracts, and licenses be written more clearly? Or are there instances in which a certain amount of ambiguity is necessary and/or unavoidable?

Seventh, in connection with any principal-agent relationship (but particularly for such "business associations" as partnerships, corporations, and limited liability companies), the trio of: **Authority, Responsibility and Liability**. That is:

- Which human beings or companies (including law firms) are authorized, explicitly or implicitly, to act on behalf of another person or company?
- To what degree are they responsible for serving that person or company rather than themselves (under their "duty of loyalty")?
- How careful (under their "duty of care") do they have to be in their service?

- If they breach either or both of these duties, are they liable to that person or company and to third parties for any damages?
- Are any of a company's managers (such as a corporation's directors and officers) or any of a company's owners (such as a company's shareholders) personally liable for harm caused by another person or another company acting on the company's behalf?

Eighth, the tensions between and the definitions distinguishing, **Insiders and Outsiders**. In *Wall Street*, which concerned insider trading, Michael Douglas's Gordon Gekko admonished his increasingly disillusioned protégé Bud Fox (Charlie Sheen), "Wake up, will you, pal? If you're not inside, you are outside, ok?"

But it's not always that clear. For instance, the "independent directors" of a company could be seen both as insiders (as members of the board) and as outsiders capable of providing disinterested perspectives (because they don't also work as officers for the company, and don't have other significant ties to it); however, in this context, "independent" has been defined in several different ways.

Is a company's senior in-house lawyer an insider or an outsider? Reflecting recent tendencies to invite and include her in its executive decision-making, some leading corporations have retitled their "General Counsel" as their "Chief Legal Officer," or CLO. (Confusingly, some companies give the same individual both titles.) To what degree can a company's outside counsel still be seen as an outsider?

Ninth, the duty of a lawyer (or client) to acquire, assimilate, and apply **Information** relevant to a legal arrangement; whether and how to create **Documentation** of legal agreements, especially for possible use as evidence in any subsequent litigation; and the **Transparency** of a company's or a government agency's operations—how much of its internal documentation must be made available to outsiders?

Tenth, the relation of the lawyer's, the client's, and society's, **Morality and ethics** to the question of what is **Legally permissible** and to the larger question of what, procedurally and substantively, constitutes **Justice**.

For instance, the American Bar Association's Model Rule of Professional Conduct 2.1, which concerns the lawyer's role as an "Advisor," allows (but does not require) her, when rendering advice, to refer "not only to law but to other [relevant] considerations such as moral, economic, social and political factors." Moreover, Rule 1.16(b)(4) generally allows the lawyer to withdraw from representing the client if "the client insists upon taking action that the lawyer considers repugnant or with which the lawyer has a fundamental disagreement."

Eleventh, the lawyer's involvement in a "meta" level of rulemaking: Just as classic literature like *The Odyssey* and *Don Quixote* might be read as stories about telling, creating, or reading stories, some court decisions, statutes, and regulations essentially construct **Rules or processes for making further rules and processes**.

Twelfth, the **Systemic interdependence and dynamics** of the caselaw, statutes, regulations, and economic and societal networks that you are studying. For instance, how do you see the law as leading and/or as responding to technological, political, social, economic, and cultural changes and their interactions?

Also, what are the tempo and speed of law's responses to change? One of the characters in Ernest Hemingway's *The Sun Also Rises* (1926), when asked how he went into bankruptcy, replied, "Two ways. . . Gradually and then suddenly." In a 2012 essay for *The New York Times*, economist Lawrence Summers, a former president of Harvard, warned readers that "[T]hings take longer to happen than you think they will, and then happen faster than you thought they could."

Even without delving into the technical field's advanced mathematics, you might find mind-expanding the analogies and perspectives in some of the recent popularizations of the study of **Complex systems**, sometimes called complex adaptive systems or dynamic systems.

The discipline addresses "self-organizing," or "emergent," patterns in the behavior of interacting participants, like birds in a flock or bees in a swarm, that could be subject to a limited number of rules. When does their interaction reach some form of equilibrium, synchronization, and/or cyclic behavior? How and when can such a system be said to be adaptive or capable of learning? How resilient is this behavior to perturbations or disruptions of the system? How and when can such a system be modeled, and its behavior predicted?

Among the most useful books on these topics for general readers are: Kevin Kelly, *Out of Control* (1992); Mitchell Waldrop, *Complexity* (1992); John H. Holland, *Emergence* (1998); and George E. Mobus and Michael C. Kalton, *Principles of Systems Science* (2015).

A final, often unacknowledged, theme of legal education is what might be called the **Non-arguability** of certain topics or issues. What personal positions might you, or others, not be prepared to surrender, no matter what arguments are made against them?

I once mentioned to another law student a news story I'd been disturbed by, about actions taken by people who belonged to a particular spiritual group. He said, "I understand why you feel that, but you probably didn't know that I'm a member of that group, and there are some things that I just won't discuss or argue about."

Chapter 7
Twenty-Two Ways in Which Law School Differs from Law Practice

Forsan et haec olim meminisse juvabit.
Perhaps one day it will please us to remember [even] these things.
Virgil, *Aeneid*

For better or worse, your law school experience, particularly if you're not involved in a legal clinic, might be much different from what you can expect in the practice of law, especially at large law firms.

First, although some legal practices might regularly be busier during some times of year than others, they don't have a semester structure, or even a special summer schedule. As a lawyer, you'll probably be working on any given day on several different projects, which didn't all begin at once and won't all end at the same time. It can be disorienting, during your first few years out of law school, not to be "resetting" all of your work in early January or in late August.

Second, in law school, you're often (if not mostly) working by yourself, unless you're involved in a clinic, a group project, a student journal, an extracurricular team in Moot Court or a transactional competition, or a study group.

Third, in law school, you generally won't have to supervise or manage the work of other people, but in practice you might well be overseeing administrative assistants, paralegals, and junior lawyers, for whose mistakes or misinterpretations you might be held at least partially responsible. Law school usually won't provide you, at least on a formal level, with training in management skills.

Fourth, in law school, you're responsible only to yourself (or perhaps your team), not to a real client, and there won't be a requirement or recording of "billable hours" to be charged to a client.

Fifth, in the classroom or during office hours, there's no penalty for asking questions (especially when exams are graded anonymously). In fact, you're encouraged to ask questions, and a good teacher will appreciate the chance to clarify a point that others might have also been wondering about.

By contrast, in practice many junior lawyers worry that asking a particular question about the facts, the law, or the nature of an assignment will diminish them before, or will annoy, a senior lawyer or a client. That concern isn't limited to lawyers: To preclude similar problems in a life-and-death context, some hospitals (as reported by the *Wall Street Journal* in August 2016) now require their newer physicians (residents) to report certain patient-related medical situations to supervising doctors.

Sixth, your teachers and classmates are usually interested not only in your answer to a question but in the process by which you reached it.

Clients, not always so much. One of my first assignments as an associate was to revise the forms that a corporate client used when selling its products. I carefully researched the relevant law, which involved a few particularly intriguing legal issues. After I telephoned a representative of the client and obtained the necessary information, I suggested, "You might be interested in why I needed to know that." He immediately said, "I don't care."

Seventh, it might be easy to forget during some class discussions of court decisions that the parties to a contract and/or litigation are real people who are directly affected by the specific legal doctrines at issue. In practice, whether or not they've got a winning case, clients are often deeply identified with their positions and their businesses. Lawyers are trained to help clients make legal, rather than business or personal, decisions. But these lines can blur: for instance, as the novel (1969) and movie (1972), *The Godfather*, repeatedly illustrate, it can be difficult to draw the line (or to believe someone who claims to have done so) between what's "business" and what's primarily "personal."

Eighth, although in law school you're usually free to draw your own conclusions in a paper or article, in a blog, or on some parts of an exam, in practice you often have a very good sense of what the client's preferred answer will be, even if that's not the conclusion that your research and analysis ultimately support.

Ninth and Tenth, the decisions and law review articles in your casebooks usually provide the relevant background information for their analyses, but in practice you're often responsible for educating yourself about a particular client's operations and those of its industry. On the other hand, casebook authors usually edit their versions of decisions to remove material that they consider peripheral; in practice, you'll be reading complete decisions and distilling their meaning for yourself and your colleagues and clients.

Eleventh, in practice, unlike law school, you might find yourself acting as a sort of translator or intermediary between, for instance, businesspeople and regulators or scientists, and helping to create some common ground between their respective professional perspectives and communities' cultures.

Twelfth, although as a law student you can often define the scope of your own research, in a law firm you might be assigned to work on only a small piece of a larger project. To the extent you reasonably can, you might try to learn about the larger scope of the project and about the client's operations and industry. That might give you a better perspective on your assignment, and help you position yourself for further work on that issue and for that client or related ones.

Thirteenth, many legal issues and the practice teams that firms have created to address them involve material taught in several different courses in the law school curriculum. For example, as discussed in Chapters 24 and 25, a law firm's ESG (Environmental, Social, and Governance) practice group often includes lawyers from not just its environmental, corporate governance, and securities groups but also from its labor/employment law and other practices, and maybe from its crisis management group.

And, of course, one client, whether a person or an organization, can generate issues in a variety of different areas. Months before UCLA Law School launched a course on "The Law of Elon Musk," I'd proposed that my law school offer a panel presentation on exactly that topic at our August 2022 orientation for incoming students (with possible follow-up programs during the academic year) to cover such cross-curricular concerns.

Fourteenth, as a law student you'll have the luxury of knowing, weeks before they take place, when and where your examinations will be, what they'll cover, the formats (essay, multiple-choice, short answer) that the questions will take, and which materials you'll be able to consult in the exam room.

An unforgettable (but practically unrealistic) way to illustrate the difference between this predictability and the circumstances of actual legal practice would be for a teacher to suddenly change, shortly before the time that an upper-class exam is scheduled to begin, not only the assigned room, but the allotted time for the exam itself, and (because some lawyers and clients expect associates to remember details of long-since-completed projects) to base parts of some questions on material from a required first-year course.

Fifteenth, although you can select many of your courses (and often have a choice of several sections of a particular course), lawyers are subject to the needs of their firms, which are driven by the shifting demands of their clients. Someone who joined one practice group at a firm might thus find herself partially or totally reassigned to another group.

Sixteenth, however imperfect law school examinations are as a means of evaluating your understanding of course material, at least you'll usually be asked the same questions as everyone else in your course. Law practice involves much muddier metrics for success.

Simply "knowing your stuff," however deeply, isn't always acknowledged, whether inside or outside one's firm; a lawyer's individual contribution to a success, whether in a litigation or a transaction, might not always be clear to or appreciated by the client, or by supervising lawyers; and a lawyer might well be unfairly blamed for a "failure," especially given the facts of the particular situation to which he was assigned.

Seventeenth, in preparing a term paper for a class, you'll be able to write a draft, set it aside, and then revise it. The pressures of law practice often demand a much faster turn-around.

In several job interviews that I had with law firms, partners looking over my résumé asked about the English essay prizes that I'd won as an undergraduate. I learned not to mention that I'd enjoyed the process of reviewing and polishing the essays: Their inevitable response was, "In practice, we often don't have the luxury of doing that." (It did cross my mind that they might be playing a mind game, and that if I'd said instead that I liked waiting for bursts of inspiration and then writing quickly, I might have received similarly distanced responses.)

Eighteenth, as suggested by the interviewers' answer, in practice you won't always have the opportunity, before a conclusion is demanded by a client, to fully research both the facts and law, and to consider the issues as carefully as you might have during a law school seminar or reading period. In fact, a hiring partner told me recently that, for this reason, she asked candidates how they felt about having to make decisions quickly. (As Lorne Michaels, the longtime producer of *Saturday Night Live*, once told a journalist, "We don't go on because we're ready: we go on because it's 11:30.") For a discussion of this situation, see Appendix C, *Fourteen Suggestions for Ethical Counseling in Fluid Situations*.

In practice, if not also in law school, you might continually consider, while engaged in research and analysis for a complex project, "If I needed to give someone my overview and (tentative) conclusion(s) right now, what would they be?"

Nineteenth, unlike in law school, you might not always be clearly told when an assignment is due (in which case, you should always ask); and, an assignment is more likely to be changed or cancelled, or to have its deadline radically shortened. In other words, like objects seen in a rear-view mirror, deadlines might be closer than they appear.

Twentieth, as noted in Chapter 5, although you might earn at least partial credit on law school exams simply for identifying the legal problems raised in their hypothetical "issue-spotter" questions, clients and senior lawyers dread the "deal-killer" who identifies a serious concern without also at least suggesting some way to resolve it.

Twenty-first, it should be acceptable, and even expected, in some classroom situations for you or your teacher to say, "I'm not certain of the answer, but I'll research it, and let you know." However, clients (especially the less legally sophisticated ones) don't always appreciate such candor or caution. A crucial but complicated skill for any junior lawyer is the ability to retain her credibility, as well as the confidence of the client, adversary, or senior lawyer with whom she's communicating, while temporarily avoiding committing herself (or her firm or client) to an immediate and definite answer.

However, at least inside a law firm, you might still be encouraged to come to a conclusion. As a summer associate between my first and second year of law school, I prepared for a partner a memo summarizing a particular client's complicated options, and their respective advantages and disadvantages. I assumed that I shouldn't presume to recommend one of those options, but the partner told me that I should have included that. He said, "We know you're a summer associate, and we'll take that into account."

Twenty-second, although lawyers (in)famously proceed with "an abundance of caution"; sometimes clarify in their documents, "for the avoidance of doubt," elements that might already seem obvious; and can adopt a deliberately redundant "belt and suspenders" approach to preventing problems, clients often have a much greater tolerance for, and might even invite and welcome, risks.

One day, after having worked with a client for hours in a conference room, I was walking him to the door of the firm's office when he remarked, "You know, I've been very, very wealthy several times, and I've also been close to personal bankruptcy several times."

Tired as I was, I couldn't stop myself from saying, "No offense, but personally, I couldn't live that way."

He grinned, and told me, "No offense to *you*, but that's why you lawyers generally don't get really, really rich."

Chapter 8
Nineteen Ways in Which Law School Resembles Law Practice

First, like a law firm, and like that portion of a state's bar that is devoted to any specialized practice (for instance, bankruptcy law), your law school's community can come to feel much smaller than it actually is.

One of my classmates told me that he went a few miles away to Boston when he took walks for relaxation, because he didn't want to be recognized by anyone.

The insular and immersive nature of law school is also emphasized by Scott Turow's 1977 book, *One L*, in which, as the year's final exams approached, the author's crucial decision involved the ethics and morality of. . . . whether to share his study group's carefully prepared outline with a classmate.

Second and Third, as in law practice, you're never necessarily "off the clock"; and you don't have to, and usually aren't expected to, "leave your work at the office."

In college, one of my friends, a molecular biology major, told me about the experiment he'd set up to run in a campus lab over the next several months. I asked, "What happens if there's a blackout, or your equipment gets knocked over?" He said, "I'd have to start all over." As a philosophy major, I felt fortunate to be able to do my reading and writing anywhere and anytime.

Of course, technology has increasingly made remote practice, and, to some degree, setting one's own schedule, more viable for lawyers. And, although there are many intriguing issues about the professional ethics of billing clients, I think that just about everyone agrees that time spent considering a client's legal issues is properly billable to that client, whatever else the lawyer might be doing (such as taking a shower) at the time.

Fourth, as in law school, personal connections might make things much easier. One day in practice, I was assigned, on very short notice, to appear in bankruptcy court to argue against a motion by opposing counsel, whom I'll call

Jack. The only other people in the courtroom were the judge, the court stenographer, and Jack, who seemed to be only a few years older than I was.

Jack made his argument, and I made mine. Then he made another argument. The judge said to the stenographer, "Off the record," and then said, "Good point, Jack." Which was not something that I'd ever seen in a movie or television show about lawyers.

Jack might have had the better legal case that morning, but after that I wasn't exactly shocked when the judge granted his motion. What did surprise me was that, when we went to the court clerk's office to have the order entered, the man behind the desk actually stood up, shook Jack's hand, and said, "Jack! How are you? How's the family?"

Fifth, in both law school and in a firm, you'll be "learning on the job."

The very best analogy that I have for legal practice from my years as an associate came from the time that a partner I'd been working with called me at home one Friday night and asked urgently, "Walter, could you be on my crew tomorrow?"

Thinking that I'd be joining one of his litigation teams, I agreed. However, I quickly found out that he'd hadn't been speaking figuratively: He was actually taking a client out sailing the next morning and wanted someone to help him handle his boat. Although I told him that I'd never been on a sailboat before, that didn't seem to matter. (Clearly, I hadn't been the first person on his call list that day, or that evening.)

The next morning, I found myself scrambling around the deck of his boat, literally "learning the ropes" as he shouted instructions, and trying to remember his warning not to get swept overboard if the boom rotated across the deck. Every now and then, when the wind died down, I could relax and appreciate the sunlight, shadows, and scenery, as well as the way the boat was gliding through the blue-green water; but then the wind would pick back up, and I'd be scrambling, and learning, again.

Sixth and Seventh, as in law school, you might have to teach yourself some material; and you might not receive, unless you ask for it, a very detailed evaluation of your work.

When I was in practice in New Jersey, I knew an associate in a prestigious large law firm in New York that was widely reputed to provide "great training" to its junior lawyers. But according to what I now heard, that "training" often consisted of associates' checking out material from the firm's library or online databases, educating themselves about new areas of the law, and getting (if they were lucky) very little feedback on the memos that they'd submitted.

Eighth, in the same way that many faculty members, particularly those teaching large classes, might not remember the names of individual students, in large firms, junior lawyers might often be mostly unknown to more senior ones.

One afternoon when I was a mid-level associate, I saw a group of summer associates down the hall and considered introducing myself. But, remembering how much work I still had to do that day, I decided that I'd just meet them when we worked on different projects together. Moments later, I realized that's probably the same attitude that some law firm partners have towards both summer associates and junior associates.

Ninth, you have to carefully do the reading, no matter how long and unexciting it is, especially if it's something that your client is relying on you to review (or might blame you for not having reviewed).

Even some law students mention not having read the digital or hard copy "terms and conditions" to which they've indicated (especially by clicking on a pop-up window) their agreement.

By contrast, a receptionist at a dentist's office was annoyed when, after she wanted me to sign a form indicating that I'd had the opportunity to review their privacy practices, I actually asked to see the document that detailed those practices. She had to dig around in a desk drawer to find a copy, which clearly had rarely been requested. Similarly, I understand that some real estate agents derisively refer to clients who insist on reviewing the legal documents themselves, rather than just "signing on the dotted line," as "readers."

Tenth, in both law school and law practice, you'll probably move from standard and traditional legal situations to those—such as many cryptocurrency-related issues—in which it's unclear, maybe even to regulatory authorities, which rules are relevant and how they apply. You might well have to extend, or at least make analogies to, established facts, law, and approaches in situations whose facts are sometimes fluid.

There's a joke that undergraduate physics majors think they know how the universe works; that as graduate students in physics they start realizing that they don't really know; and that by the time they receive their PhDs, they understand that nobody else knows, either. As a law student you can progress from carefully briefing decisions and making outlines in your first-year courses to taking upper-level seminars on, or pursuing independent studies of, topics for which a comprehensive outline might not yet be possible.

Eleventh, both lawyers and law students should always be alert for and learning about the new legal issues and areas created by technological, business, social, and cultural developments.

Twelfth, neither law students nor practicing lawyers can afford not to know and not to heed the rules of professional responsibility.

Although in various movies and television series a veteran police officer advises his rookie partner to disregard "what they taught you in the academy," lawyers do so at their own professional peril—particularly since a client who demands that her lawyer cut ethical corners might end up turning on (and/or turning in) her own counsel. (Like medical students, doctors, and lawyers, law students might want to emphasize, whether online or at social events, that any of their responses to a question about someone's personal situation should not be construed as professional advice.)

Thirteenth, not just law schools but law firms and courts have unwritten, often unmentioned, but sometimes essential, rules, standards, and customs known by second- and third-year students (or, by administrative assistants, more experienced lawyers, and court clerks).

Fourteenth, more generally, both law students and lawyers can always benefit from mentors, whether those are faculty members or senior students (or senior lawyers), or even current or former clients. A regular weekend feature of the *Wall Street Journal* is its depiction of a businessperson's personal "board of directors"—that is, the four or five individuals to whom that person turns for professional advice (although, unlike a corporation's board, they generally seem to be consulted individually and informally). Which of your law school teachers would you consider to be, or like to be, a mentor? Which do you think you might want to stay in touch with after graduation?

Fifteenth, in both law school and legal practice, administrators might not be so insensitive as you might imagine, and there could be valid reasons behind seemingly arbitrary practices.

As a first-year student, long before schools could make final grades available online, I heard many complaints from 2Ls and 3Ls about having had to line up in a classroom to receive their fall semester grades, especially since many couldn't resist opening their grade report, and reacting to it, in front of everyone else. That problem (although nine years earlier) had even been discussed in *One L*.

As my section's student government representative, I suggested to the Registrar's Office that fall grades, like spring grades, might simply be mailed. They told me that when they'd tried that some years previously, students had complained because the letters were delivered to some students later than to others. But as I recall, we arranged for a mailing option and also for more rooms (and thus shorter lines) in which students could receive their grades.

Sixteenth, every law student thinks about positioning herself to find a good job. But not every student, at least when I was in law school, considered that the same is true in legal practice. Probably only a small percentage of law school graduates will spend their careers with their first employer, so developing one's skills, reputation, and professional portfolio, especially with an eye towards their "portability" to another firm and/or geographic region, will enable you to make the next transition more smoothly. (I once read that helicopter pilots are trained to identify, at any moment they're aloft, where they'd try to land if there were an emergency.)

Seventeenth (as discussed in Chapter 21), both law school and legal practice can be physically and mentally stressful.

Eighteenth, just as the specific questions asked on an exam might not allow a law student to demonstrate the depth of her command of the material or the hours that she spent studying, so can the choice of questions asked by the court during oral argument or the ways in which a particular transaction is shaped and implemented deny a lawyer the opportunity to demonstrate (even to clients, who might object to that portion of the legal fees) the plethora of possibilities for which she professionally and painstakingly prepared.

Nineteenth, neither law students nor lawyers wear any special clothing, or use any distinctive professional equipment—with the possible exceptions of legal pads and of "trial bags" (also known as "litigation cases," and often carried by traveling salespeople).

Although at many law schools, orientation for entering students now includes some form of oath or pledge of professionalism, the occasion doesn't introduce an item in the way that a medical school's "white coat ceremony," during which students might recite the Hippocratic Oath, involves their donning that garment to mark the beginning of their training.

(Many believe that the distinctive feature of "legal pads" is their length—14 inches rather than 11—but it's actually the red vertical line 1 ¼ inches from the left edge of the page. I never learned the special significance or use of that line for lawyers, but maybe I missed that part of my own 1L orientation.)

Chapter 9
Getting (Fully) Oriented

Although some of the following items might be addressed before or during your school's formal orientation program, you might want to add some of the others to your settling-in list for the first week of classes.

First, if you expect to need any type of counseling, or any physical or other accommodations in attending classes, taking notes, and/or taking exams—or if you anticipate that during the year you might miss classes because of a personal or family health situation or other serious matter—let the Student Affairs and other relevant office(s) know. In discussing the types of assistance that might be available, you should be able to rely on their discretion (both in the sense of their judgment and in the sense of their maintaining confidentiality).

Second, visit the law library and introduce yourself to the reference librarians, who are among any law school's unsung heroes. Not only can they identify and help you obtain an enormous amount of online and hard copy resources for your research (and, maybe, your job search), but their advice and insights can save you extraordinary amounts of time and energy.

Third, ask the librarians how to use the school's interlibrary loan (ILL) system, which is probably available through the library's Web site, and through which you can borrow many useful books for research purposes.

Fourth, ask them how you can find, and download for free, legal pleadings (complaints, answers, motions, and other litigation documents filed by the parties) in litigation currently before different courts (including some high-profile bankruptcy cases). As discussed in Chapters 13 and 28, just browsing through some of those real-life examples can lend new dimensions to your class preparation and to your job interviews.

Fifth, browse in the library's "stacks," particularly those corresponding to the areas of law you're interested in. Just as in a good used bookstore, you might be surprised at what you discover, and one book or topic could even change your life.

Sixth, if access isn't limited to library staff, take a look at the items on the shelves of the "reserve section." Many libraries lend, even if only for a few hours' use at a time within the library itself, popular study aids, treatises, and casebooks (possibly including all of the leading casebooks for many courses). You could also ask the circulation desk librarians which of these books are the most popular.

Seventh, ask the librarians whether and how you might be able as a law student to get free online access to *The New York Times*, *The Wall Street Journal*, and the *Washington Post* (and maybe, if you're particularly interested in business law, the *Financial Times*). Also, if you'd like to work in a particular city or region, you might check on the availability of its newspaper(s) through the library's Web site, or see if the publications' Web sites offer a student rate for online subscriptions.

Eighth, learn from the librarians (who might have posted and/or offer during the academic year presentations on such topics) at least the basics of how to use the library's online catalog to find books and articles.

Although being able to use the finer features of common programs and applications can come in handy, in the workplace you might not want to be known as the go-to person for everyone's Word or Excel problems. On the other hand, a reputation for resourcefulness in online research could well bring you welcome attention from even—and maybe especially—senior partners, particularly during a client's emergency. (You might even, every now and then, call the Westlaw and/or Lexis customer support numbers to ask whether there are any new resources or features relevant to your research and career interests.)

Ninth, ask the librarians if the library posts online any previous exams for the first-semester courses you're taking. If so, download and browse through them, just to get a sense of the types of questions that are asked and of recurring issues and themes. (See also the exam-preparation discussion in Chapter 16.)

Tenth, visit the ABA's Web site (americanbar.org) and, if you haven't already, consider joining the organization and as many of its sections and committees as sound interesting to you.

Even if you don't agree with all of ABA's public positions on legal and social issues, law student membership, which is low-cost or free, will open a spigot to a steady flow of extremely practical and practice-oriented material on a wide range of emerging topics and concerns. Moreover, many of the ABA's sections, committees, subcommittees, and working groups are happy to welcome law students as active participants in their ongoing work, which can be a very productive opportunity for both learning and networking. Their specialized law reviews, magazines, and newsletters can also provide many opportunities for publication. (Don't forget to add these memberships and activities to your résumé.)

Also, on the pages for the ABA sections you're interested in, check for upcoming physical (or hybrid) meetings, which are usually held in hotels in major cities and which offer, beyond information-rich presentations, extraordinary possibilities for networking.

Eleventh, you might similarly contact the bar associations of the states (and cities) in which you're considering working, to see whether you can join as a student member. Even if they have no formal policies on, or limit or don't allow, student involvement, you might be able to subscribe to hard copy or digital versions of their regular publication(s) at a discounted rate or for free. In any event, as with the ABA, you can find online the names of the leaders of the bar sections that interest you and contact them directly with questions about paper topics and career advice.

Twelfth, consider joining the American Bankruptcy Institute (abi.org) as a student member. Like the ABA, this nonpartisan group of lawyers, judges, and academics offers a wide variety of information (including, through their online bookstore, dozens of books for practitioners), opportunities for participation, and educational meetings. (Chapter 27 discusses the advantages of studying and practicing bankruptcy law.)

Thirteenth, although it might seem premature, make appointments to talk with the directors of the law school's programs, departments, clinics, or concentrations whose descriptions on the school's Web site or in other publications attract you. You might be able to find out more about the programs' goals and operations, the opportunities they offer, and how to prepare for and apply to them; and, they'll be aware of your interest.

Fourteenth (sadly), check the emergency evacuation routes from your classrooms, and whether (and how) their doors can be locked from the inside. You might also note where the fire extinguishers, AEDs (automated external defibrillators), and any emergency telephones are located, and save for quick reference the emergency and non-emergency phone numbers of the local and campus police.

Fifteenth, buy a printed newspaper on the first day of your orientation, and/or your first day of classes. Save at least the front page. It might not seem like a big thing at the time, but when you graduate (another good day to buy a newspaper), this low-cost time capsule will provide some historical and cultural perspective on your journey.

Sixteenth, talk with the Career Services office about advice for finding employment in areas of practice in which you're interested, and about whether there are any restrictions on when you might start contacting potential employers.

If it's not already on your law school's Web site, you could request a copy of the recruiting policies that they expect employers to comply with (concerning, for example, how long offers should remain open).

As background information, you could ask which legal fields are, and are expected to be over the next few years, the most in demand; and, what resources (in addition to the Web site of the National Association for Law Placement, nalp.org) they would recommend that you monitor.

Also, you could give them a copy of your résumé and ask if they have any suggestions for editing or formatting it.

Seventeenth, visit the school's Information Technology group, even if your laptop and smartphone are already appropriately configured, to see if they have any extra advice and to explore what other services they might provide. For instance, if something suddenly goes wrong with your laptop, is there a way that the law school will let you sign out a spare laptop for temporary use? Are there any programs or apps that they recommend that you download, possibly for free or at a student discount? If you need to buy or rent a computer, do they have any specific recommendations or know about any discounts available to students (either through your school or in general)?

Eighteenth, consider reserving, through a domain name registrar like GoDaddy.com, "dot-com" domain names corresponding to your name.

For instance, years ago I reserved the names effross.com, waltereffross.com, and walter-effross.com. Even if you're not going to use the addresses immediately—such as, for a blog, or to automatically forward visitors (as I did with effross.com) to a page with a much more complicated address—it might not cost that much to make sure that you'll be able to use the names if and when you decide to. During your law school career, you might also consider reserving other domain names, especially if you're planning to blog about any law-related topics.

Chapter 10
Assumpsit: A Word About Dictionaries

Although you might not find your law school experience to be quite like, as some have claimed, learning a new language, it will certainly expand your English and Latin vocabularies.

When I began law school, second-year students advised me not to buy the classic, authoritative, and hefty *Black's Law Dictionary*, saying that I probably wouldn't use it very much.

I was prepared to take their advice, until I read one of the very first words of the first case assigned for my first class—the *Hawkins v. McGee*, or "hairy hand," decision (84 N.H. 114, 146 A. 641 (N.H. 1929)), immortalized as the focus of Professor Kingsfield's stern Socratization of a woefully unprepared James Hart early in the novel and movie *The Paper Chase*.

When I saw that word—"Assumpsit"—I went right out and bought that dictionary.

As it turned out, the 2Ls had been absolutely correct: I didn't use the dictionary much more during law school (even though in the mid-1980s we didn't have the Internet to look up definitions).

Today, if you'd like to invest in a hard-copy legal dictionary, I'd suggest the much more affordable and easily portable paperback *Merriam-Webster's Dictionary of the Law* (2016), which includes helpful appendices on The Judicial System, Important Cases, Important Laws, and Important Agencies.

You might also consider acquiring another paperback, *The Merriam-Webster Dictionary of Synonyms and Antonyms* (1994), which, instead of simply listing alternate or opposite terms as a thesaurus does, carefully explains the sometimes subtle differences among groups of words that have similar but not identical meanings. If words are the colors that lawyers paint with, this book will help you find the most appropriate shades.

(If you're interested, you can find online discussions of why that publisher's *Webster's New International Dictionary* (2d ed. 1934), often referred to as "Webster's Second"—and sometimes still available from booksellers, though not inexpensively—is preferred by a number of word aficionados to *Webster's Third New International Dictionary* (1961).)

Finally, you might find of use Deborah E. Bouchoux's *Aspen Handbook for Legal Writers: A Practical Reference* (5th ed. 2021), a very handy guide to the syntax, structure, style, and citation forms of legal writing.

Chapter 11
Eight Useful Supplies

You might find it helpful to color-code your courses and projects and to use correspondingly colored manila files, clipboards, notebooks, and 3-ring binders for each.

A few relatively inexpensive, and mostly low-tech, items that could make your life easier are:

First, a Pendaflex or Smead 1-31 expanding "desk file/sorter" is a durable cover around 31 heavy-duty tabbed pages, so that you can separate loose documents by day of the month—or into whatever categories you'd like. You could tape a numbered list of your own categories onto the front cover.

Second, although you may already be storing documents in "the cloud," a variety of flash/thumb drives and external drives could be easy insurance, especially if you regularly (perhaps weekly) alternate your backup drives and if you store some of those backups in different locations.

Third, you might keep a good supply of the humble, old-school index card, whether 3x5 inches or 4x6 inches, to use as bookmarks or note cards, or for making some of the lists discussed in Chapter 12, and (perhaps cut in half) the flash cards discussed in Chapter 13.

Fourth, a four-color retractable ballpoint pen could come in handy for diagramming or taking notes on complex issues. (You might have used such a pen if you took Organic Chemistry as an undergraduate; I remember the waves of clicking sounds that spread across the room when the teacher started drawing molecular diagrams on the board.)

Fifth, a small (about thumb-long) utility knife with a blade that retracts into the body of the knife is useful not only for clipping articles from publications but also (although this may be unthinkable for some) removing particular pages to save from books that you're preparing to recycle or discard.

Sixth, even if your primary calendar is on your phone or online, a paper calendar can be a great backup to note important appointments, reminders, and contact and emergency information. I recommend the At-A-Glance DayMinder

Academic Weekly Planner, which measures about 3 ½ by 6 inches and covers July through June.

Seventh, it's always good to have a pen and pad available, especially in a professional environment and also on your nightstand.

Eighth, 50-quart stackable Sterilite brand (or similar) translucent plastic "totes" (tubs) with latching lids could protect your books, files, and loose papers better than paper boxes or even filing cabinets.

You might be surprised at some of the other items available in hardware and stationery stores. Browsing through those aisles (or through the stores' Web sites) could also stimulate creative ideas, or material for analogies, to help solve other problems.

Chapter 12
Four More Core Lists

We do not receive wisdom, we must discover it for ourselves, after a journey through the wilderness, which no one else can make for us, which no one can spare us, for our wisdom is the point of view from which we come at last to view the world.

Marcel Proust, *Remembrance of Things Past*

From the very beginning of your law school journey, you might consider constructing, in addition to the lists discussed in Chapter 2, four different (digital or hard copy) lists, collections, or compilations.

None of the four is a "to-do" list as such; nor does any have to become a full-fledged journal (although, if you're interested in maintaining one of those, I recommend Kathleen Adams' *Journal to the Self* (1990) and Christina Baldwin's *Life's Companion* (1990)).

In fact, although you could divide any of the four into subsidiary lists, none has to be especially complex, elaborate, or high-tech. As noted in Chapter 11, you might even keep and organize some of them on index cards.

Individually and together, they could save you much time and mental energy, and become personal archives, intellectual maps, and professional resources, through your law school years and beyond.

First, set up the equivalent of a **Commonplace Book** (a genre whose long history and most prominent practitioners are detailed in Wikipedia's page on the topic) to record and date the especially notable remarks, thoughts, incidents, excerpts from readings, and other items that you'd like to remember and preserve.

For example, during my first year, when I heard that a parent of one of my section's professors had died, I circulated a condolence card around the room for signatures and left it on his lectern before he came in for the next class. He picked it up and read it, looked up at us, and said, softly and simply, "Thank you," before starting his lecture.

That might not seem like a major event, but it was a rare moment in which I felt strongly that, beyond the teacher-student relationship, we were all just human beings together in a law school classroom.

Second, maintain a collection of **References and Research** to follow up on (including notes about issues that you might want to write or blog about), whether those are to books, articles, Web sites, people and companies to contact, or trends that you've noticed.

As part of this list, you could record and date the terms and scope of the searches that you conduct on legal databases like Westlaw and Lexis-Nexis, to save you from inadvertently duplicating your work and to make it easier to update your research later.

You could also record the titles of the books you read, as you finish reading them, and copy down any reactions to, or references in, those books that you might like to follow up on.

Third, keep an **ABC List** of **Arguments, Building Blocks, and Clauses** (some of which may also appear in other fields, such as rhetoric and economics) that you encounter in your classes and assigned reading.

- When are different modes of argument (including conflicting methods of interpreting statutes and regulations)—like "the slippery slope," the "original intent," and the "plain meaning"— most effective?
- What are the respective counter-arguments?
- What basic concepts, archetypes, and themes—like "good faith," "the reasonable person," "the tragedy of the commons," "moral hazard," "intent," the "independence" of a corporate director (or other agent), "efficiency," and "externalities"—appear in different contexts?
- How do these concepts and arguments relate to, connect, combine with, or maybe oppose, each other? Can they be grouped or categorized, like the families of some elements in chemistry's periodic table?
- What types of specialized clauses and provisions appear in the contracts, licenses, and other arrangements that you're studying, and what purposes do they serve?

For example, after litigation established that the license to publish a hard-copy version of a book did not automatically include the right to publish digital versions, publishers' lawyers began amending licenses to cover publishing rights "in all technologies now known or hereinafter invented."

Other examples include "morality clauses" governing the conduct of performers, product endorsers, and even corporate executives; and terms addressing a content creator's "moral rights" to enable her to control the way in which her work is displayed (such as by allowing her to prevent the colorization of an image or video created in black and white), to insist on a certain form of attribution, or even to demand that one of her works be attributed to a pseudonym (as apparently has been a practice of some movie directors, who might use for this purpose the name "Alan Smithee").

The fourth list is of material related to **Words and Wordsmithing**. Beyond definitions of useful words, you might include:

- Particularly interesting etymologies (easily found on Merriam-Webster's Web site, m-w.com), which can illuminate a word's meaning, help fix that meaning in your mind, and provide some colorful historical perspective (see, for instance, the "backstories" of "bylaws" and of "tribunal").
- "Danger words," which should be used with caution (or perhaps not at all) because they are capable of opposed or confusing constructions. These would include such "Janus words" (or, autoantonyms) as "sanction" and "oversight." (For a triple ambiguity, see the definition of "livid," which, depending on the context, could indicate that something is red, or white, or blue.)
- Common words that are used in specialized senses by lawyers: for instance, a "record," a "writing," and a "signature."
- Words that even lawyers could use for several different concepts, like "proxy" and "equity."
- What one of my first-year professors called "weasel words": deliberately imprecise terms (like "appropriate," "reasonable," and "substantial") that, if part of a contract or other agreement, might invite litigation.
- Particularly interesting, compelling, well-written, poorly written, and/or objectionable phrases, sentences, and contract provisions; and references to articles that you found (even if you didn't agree with their conclusions) especially well-crafted.
- Responses useful to someone (like a politician or an executive) who's being questioned, criticized, or blamed (for example, the re/misdirecting remark, "I think that the important thing to remember is. . . .").
- Introductions to investigative questions, such as those posed by a Congressional committee or by a lawyer taking a deposition or examining a witness (for instance, "Is it your understanding that. . . ."; "Is that consistent with. . ."; and "How would you characterize. . . .").
- Sentences and paragraphs that might appear at first to convey information but were in fact artfully designed to contain very little, or no, substance (the verbal equivalent of a small decaf skim milk coffee). A special subcategory might be instances of supposed apologies that, possibly through the artful use of the passive voice (such as, "Mistakes were made" or, among the famous first lines of Dante's *Inferno*, "the straight way was lost"), fail to convey clearly either admission or contrition.

Other lists, sub-lists, or records that you might begin making during law school include:

- A list of your contributions, achievements, and accomplishments during law school, even if many of the items might not be significant enough to add to the limited space on your résumé. (If you need more room on your résumé to include your achievements or distinctions, I'd suggest omitting any discussion of how a particular position might benefit you.)
- A "decision-making journal" reflecting on the processes you (or others) are using or have used to come to personal and professional decisions and—even if the results were successful—how you (or they) might optimize those methods in the future. See also Appendix B, *Enhancing the Decision-Making Process*.
- A list of your own and/or others' maxims, adages, aphorisms, proverbs, epigrams, or apothegms (the differences among which are not always clear) for law school, legal practice, and life.

  Anthologies of such sayings, as well as classic compilations of those written by (Francois VI, Duc de) La Rochefoucauld, Pascal, and Goethe, among others, are easily available. For a thought-provoking and contemporaneous collection by the former executive editor of *Wired* magazine, see Kevin Kelly's *Excellent Advice for Living* (2022) (some of whose entries are also available on his blog, kk.org/thetechnium).

  In a twelfth-season (2014-2015) episode of the CBS television show *NCIS*, Agent Tim McGee wondered, of the ever-growing list of principles enunciated by his team's veteran leader, "Rules Number 3, 8, 36, and 40 are the same thing. And with two Rule Number 1's, and two Rule Number 3's, I'm starting to wonder: is [Special Agent Leroy Jethro] Gibbs making up these rules as he goes?" A list of "Gibbs' Rules" is available at cbs.com/shows/ncis/photos/1003066/gibbs-rules-the-complete-list-from-ncis/.
- A list or journal of the ways that you found most effective for assimilating and studying—and for conveying to different audiences—different types of complex material.
- How you're feeling about your law school experience, perhaps including how you believe that your thinking process is changing or has changed (as discussed in Chapter 5) and the ways in which you believe you're making (and/or could be making more) progress.
- Extracurricular activities that you'd like to pursue in the area when you find the time (as discussed in Chapter 21).
- The material in your studies that you're finding most surprising and/or unfair. For me, that would have included the first-year torts doctrine that, normally, innocent bystanders have no legal duty to attempt to help someone in distress.

- The ways in which some of your class material reflects or applies to situations in the news—and, perhaps by analogy, to situations in your personal or professional life.
- Types of professional certifications that you might be interested in pursuing (and in adding to your résumé) in practice or even before graduation: for instance, in cybersecurity, privacy, parliamentary procedure, or coding. On its Web site, the American Bar Association lists "ABA Accredited Lawyer Certification Programs."
- As noted in Chapter 18, a drafting/editing/proofreading checklist, not just for articles that you might write for publication but also for legal documents that you might prepare or edit in law school and in practice. Lawyers (among whom "Good catch!" can, in this context, be considered a high compliment) are notorious noticers of typographical errors, which (especially on a résumé) can immediately call into question an author's professionalism.

  As a beginning exercise in the E-Commerce Law & Drafting course that I developed, I hand out a copy of a short but deliberately flawed software license agreement. One of the most obvious errors isn't always found the most quickly: The numbering of the provisions skips from 3 to 5.

  Such a discovery would certainly trouble a law firm partner, a client, or opposing counsel, not only because of the drafter's apparent carelessness but also because it suggests that the document might have been quickly adapted from a form, or from an agreement created for a previous transaction. The misnumbering raises the questions of what the possibly deleted provision said, why it was removed, and whether that deletion was appropriate.

  As that course progresses, we develop a checklist of drafting issues, an abbreviated version of which is reproduced as Appendix D, *A Sample/Starter Checklist for Drafting/Editing/Proofreading*.
- Finally, you might find of use the daily practice of writing "morning pages," prescribed by and discussed in Julia Cameron's best-seller, *The Artist's Way* (2002): "Three pages of whatever crosses your mind—that's all there is to it."

Chapter 13
Engaging in, Taking Notes During, and Preparing for Class

I still remember which one of my law school classmates finally volunteered to answer the first question in our first class.

Particularly during your first year, speaking in class, whether it's asking a question or being called on (with or without warning), can be particularly stressful.

No one wants to say something that could "go viral" and/or be recalled at reunions years later. On the other hand, even many people who think they know the answer don't want to look too eager. And, as discussed at length by lawyer Susan Cain in her reassuring book *Quiet: The Power of Introverts in a World That Can't Stop Talking* (2012), some law students, however intelligent and well-prepared, might be less inclined than others to speak up, especially to "shoot from the hip" in answering a surprise question. (By contrast, during Cain's research visit to Harvard Business School, a student warned her, "Good luck finding an introvert around here.")

It doesn't help that the Socratic method, although law professors might no longer employ it as commonly or intensely as in decades past, often moves from innocent-sounding questions to very tricky follow-ups, some of which, like *Star Trek II: The Wrath of Khan*'s infamous *Kobayashi Maru* exercise, might not have any "correct" answer. In the movie *The Paper Chase*, Professor Kingsfield proclaimed to his students, "You may at times think you have reached a correct and final answer. I assure you this is a delusion on your part. . . . In my classroom, there is always another question. There is always a question to follow your answer."

Some ways to make your class participation more manageable include:

First, remember that, even in courses in which class participation might affect your grade, it's often the quality rather than the quantity of your contributions that counts. Also, that participation could well include your asking perceptive questions.

Second, in many classes, students are allowed to "pass" at least once when called on. Some teachers want to be notified before class if, for any reason, a student doesn't want to be called on that day. Beyond the policies in place in your particular courses, if, because of personal circumstances or generally, you're concerned about being "cold-called" rather than being assigned in advance to discuss a particular item on the syllabus, consider talking with the teacher about it.

Third, remember that probably just about every lawyer has been embarrassed by something he or she said in a first-year class. By your second semester, and certainly by your second year, when everyone knows each other better, you and your classmates will be less concerned about having a possibly inartful answer remembered for life.

Fourth, don't necessarily take a teacher's questions at face value. If you're asked what you suspect to be a loaded question or trick question, you should identify or ask for elaboration of what you believe to be its underlying assumptions, and discuss whether you think those are correct.

Similarly, whether or not it's intended, a question or statement might depend on colloquial or legal terms that you could clarify. For instance, "If by 'efficient,' you mean, [X], then my answer would be [Y]."

Fifth, although the Socratic method often involves the teacher's changing the "facts" of a hypothetical example to test your application, interpretation, or understanding of a rule (just as, during oral arguments, judges question and challenge lawyers), don't be afraid to invent and ask about such variations yourself.

Sixth, especially when asking questions of that type, be prepared to hear, "What do *you* think the answer is?" and to propose and defend an answer of your own.

Seventh, even if you're less than certain, consider, as part of your training, answering with assurance. (On the other hand, you don't have to take it to the level that I once saw on the news: When asked, during Fire Prevention Week, "How many matches does it take to start a fire that could burn down your house?" a small boy gave the interviewer a look that conveyed, "I can't believe I really have to explain to an adult something this obvious!" and, with absolute conviction, held up the corresponding number of fingers and announced, "Six!")

Eighth, unless you have a particular reason to believe otherwise, don't take a trick/loaded question or other Socratic experience personally. Even if you didn't get the right answer, if you learned how to reach the right one, you came out ahead.

Ninth, don't be afraid to ask—if not in class, then during office hours—for further explanation. If you're not sure that you understood something, some of your classmates might be wondering about that point themselves. If you're concerned about identifying yourself as the person raising the issue, you might e-mail or talk to the teacher's administrative assistant and ask him to forward, without including your name, your question(s).

(A brief digression on the "impostor syndrome," in which people privately doubt their qualifications for their positions, offices, or other roles. During our first semester, a classmate told me quietly about having recently checked with the admissions office, because of his suspicion—which turned out to be completely unfounded—that his LSAT score had been inaccurately reported to the school as higher than his actual score, and that he shouldn't have been admitted. As far as I know, he ended up doing just fine. Members of admissions committees take their responsibilities very seriously. But I suppose that almost every law student doubts his or her capabilities at some point.)

Tenth, although it might be tempting to tune out when someone else is answering a question, instead of just waiting to hear the teacher's reaction to that answer, you should consider, and compare with her response, how you would have answered.

Eleventh, whether or not it counts towards class participation for purposes of your course grade, you might answer by e-mail if the teacher forwards to the class a news article or a link to a relevant item. It's certainly not required, but even a brief and thoughtful response could help distinguish you, without ever being noticed by your classmates. (Of course, if you'd prefer that your name not be mentioned in class in connection with those communications, you should include that in your message.)

Twelfth, in addition to the "intention" practice suggested in Chapter 2, you might consider making a habit of taking a few "mindful" or "centering" breaths at the beginning of class to help you focus. I do that immediately before every class that I teach.

Thirteenth, remember that, even more than during live theatrical or musical performances, class sessions depend on the dynamics among everyone in the room, not just the people on the stage or behind the lectern. (One of the best and most memorable classes that I ever taught was a makeup session attended by only one student, because he was completely prepared to go through the assigned material in depth. I almost felt sorry for the other members of the class, who'd have to catch up with us later by watching the recording.)

In each course and every class session, you and your classmates are not a mere audience for a series of lecturers but a community that will collectively create its own unique mood and personality. Each of you can help shape it.

How should you prepare for class?

Before the pandemic forced classes online, where services like Zoom can generate transcripts automatically, much was written about whether allowing laptops into the classroom was turning some students into stenographers rather than active listeners and participants.

I think that the key to making the most out of your classroom experience, whether it's in-person or online, is to have done the reading and prepared your own notes, even if they're not elaborate or complete. That way you won't feel the need to write everything down during class but instead can pay particular attention to points and perspectives that weren't covered or emphasized in the assigned material. (For a Torts class in the middle of my first semester, I felt completely attuned to and in command of the reading assigned, only to have the professor start the session by asserting that one of those cases had, in his view at least, been decided incorrectly.)

During your first year, preparing for class by "briefing a case"—that is, reviewing in detail its procedural posture, the facts of the situation that it addresses, and the substantive rule, or "holding," that it sets out—trains you to identify the most important aspects of a decision. In-class discussion should focus on these elements, and in particular on the holding's limits, exceptions, and ambiguities.

As part of preparing for class, you could even look online for the types of contracts, licenses, forms, or court filings that the assigned material discusses. Even if they aren't all perfect examples, just going through these real-life documents can give you a better sense of the issues involved and of the lawyer's role in addressing them.

As discussed in Chapter 15, you should incorporate into your class outline the most important parts of your class notes, as well as of any notes you've made of your reflections or reactions to the material, including during office hours. If you do this regularly, refining and reviewing your outline at the end of the semester to prepare for exams should be much simpler.

During the semester, you might also put onto flash cards some of the key rules and cases, for easy review during spare moments. Even if your exam will be open book, making and using the flash cards could help you recall the information more easily and give you the opportunity to think about and synthesize it more carefully.

Finally, for further information, clarification, or elaboration, you could always e-mail your questions to the author(s) of your casebook or of assigned law review articles. You might not hear back—but then again, you might be very pleasantly surprised.

Chapter 14
Five Secret Words for Success (and Five Reasons Why)

"When are your office hours?"

If I could give just one piece of advice to every law student, it would be to visit—not every one of, but regularly—their teachers' office hours.

One of the deans I've worked with often used the 1970s phrase, "creating a space," as in "opening an opportunity" for something. I'd recommend that you consider faculty office hours such a space or opportunity, even, and maybe especially, if you and your teacher are the only ones there.

First, during those unstructured meetings, you can introduce yourself and discuss your interests. If you have a particular background or experience, a teacher might call on you in class to add to the discussion of a certain issue.

Second, although it might be easier to send your questions about the course material by e-mail, an actual live discussion (whether in the same room or virtually) will probably be a better way to clarify your concerns and to ask any follow-up questions. Beyond helping you to better understand the course material, your teacher might appreciate your questions as a signal to review with the class, and possibly refine his presentation of, those topics.

Third, even if you don't have questions about the substantive material, faculty members can offer you career advice, discuss possible topics for papers (including perennial as well as emerging practice issues in their fields), and suggest books, articles, and Web sites to read and other people to talk with.

For these purposes, you might want to visit the office hours even of teachers whose courses you're not currently enrolled in—and maybe even of faculty in other units of your university, such as the business school.

Fourth, if you ever need to ask a teacher for a letter of recommendation to support your application for a position, that person should be able to do more than mention your grade in the course (which will already be on your transcript) and repeat a few items from your résumé (which, during their office hours, you might also ask your teachers to review).

Once, a student asked me to write a recommendation for her judicial clerkship application, even though I'd told her that I wouldn't be able to provide much more information than her grade in my course.

About a week later, I received a phone call from the judge, who was very interested in hiring the student but wanted to know, possibly because he suspected that I was trying to signal a problem that I didn't want to put in writing, why my letter of recommendation had been so brief. I explained the situation, and I privately gave the judge a lot of credit for checking.

Fifth, you might get a better sense of your professors "offstage," and maybe of the ways in which they've integrated the lessons from their teaching and research into their own lives.

During my freshman year in college, the small-group meetings of the Shakespeare course met in the teacher's office, where floor-to-ceiling bookshelves displayed dozens of the distinctively bound Norton Critical Editions of literary classics. In many of those sessions, I thought, "What must it be like to have read, and thought deeply about, all of those books?"

Later, as a philosophy major, I often wondered during those classes how my teachers' professional pursuits and publications reflected, and had shaped, their personal perspectives.

Chapter 15
Thirteen Tips for Constructing Course Outlines

Refining into outline form your class notes and your summaries of and observations on the readings is a crucial step in mastering the course material. Often-overlooked, though, is that the process itself can be just as valuable as the final product.

First, you should regard your outline as a tool for a specific purpose: helping you to perform at your best, especially under time pressure, on the exam for the course. Instead of being an encyclopedic or comprehensive treatment of the subject, it should focus on the particular issues, cases, provisions, and policies addressed during the semester.

Second, make sure that you know what material you'll be responsible for on the exam:

- Are you expected to know everything that was assigned on the syllabus or only the material that was actually covered during class sessions?
- Are you expected to be familiar with that material only to the degree to which it was discussed in class?
- Are you expected to know in detail the information in any supplemental materials (possibly including news articles) distributed during the semester, or were these intended to be "browse only"?

Third, keep in mind while preparing your outline the exam's "terms and conditions" (often announced during the beginning of the semester):

- What material can you consult during the exam—anything? only the assigned readings?
- Will you be allowed to use an outline that you've contributed a piece to but didn't write all by yourself?
- Will you be allowed to use a printed-out copy only or will you be able to access digital versions of your outline and of the course materials?

- If you can use a digital version of your outline, will you be allowed to cut and paste material from it into your exam answers?
- Will you be able to word-search through your outline? If not, you might prepare a table of contents, index, or other handy reference guide to it.
- What will be the format of the questions—essay, multiple choice, short answer, or some combination?
- Are you expected to cite caselaw, statutes, and regulations in your answers? If so, how detailed should your references be? Is there a required format for citations?
- Are your answers required to follow any specific format (such as IRAC, Issue-Rule-Analysis [or, Application]-Conclusion)?
- In answering "hypothetical questions" that involve fact patterns, are you expected to address possible policy arguments, or is there a separate section or question of the exam that will focus on such arguments?
- Can you do well by analyzing a few issues in great detail, or are you expected to identify every issue even if you don't have the time to explore all of them in depth?

Fourth, you might start making your outline relatively early in the semester, not only to enhance your understanding of the course's foundations and identify areas that you'd like to ask questions about but also to avoid time pressure during reading period.

Fifth, consider including in your outline, or preparing as separate documents, one of more of the following:

- A list associating with particular legal issues specific "fact patterns" that arise in the readings, class discussions, and previous exams.
- A list or flowchart of issues that often arise in connection with, or as alternatives to, each other.

For instance, in the Business Associations course, ways in which the personal liability of directors might be limited or precluded include: the business judgment rule, exculpation, indemnification, and directors' and officers' (D&O) insurance. An abbreviated form of another portion of a Business Associations outline, which is also applicable in other contexts (including, as noted in Chapter 24, to the governance of student organizations), appears in Appendix E, *Policies, Procedures, and Practices for Decision-Making by Voting*.

I imagine that these considerations would be like, for medical students, learning the possible medical conditions of patients who display certain symptoms, and the follow-up questions, tests, or other information needed to clarify the diagnostic possibilities and to suggest specific forms of treatment.

- A list summarizing the larger themes of the course, including policy arguments and considerations and the ways in which the caselaw, statutes, and regulations have evolved.

As the last question on my own final exams, I always include a general statement (for example, "The law of business associations, as indicated by the statutory provisions and court decisions that we have studied, has become simpler over time"), and then ask, "Do you agree, partially agree, or disagree with this statement? Discuss, citing specific statutory sections and caselaw to support your analysis." Of course, that question is deliberately designed to have more than one "correct" answer and to give each student the opportunity to crystallize the course in his or her own way around the specified "seed crystal." Your own outline might include similar statements and your responses.

Sixth, to help you master both the substantive material and the outlining process, consider constructing at least a draft of your outline, or some sections of it, before looking at commercial outlines or those prepared by students in earlier semesters of the course (or by other members of your class).

Seventh, towards the end of the course and after completing a first draft of your outline you might browse through, if they're available in the law library or if you can borrow them from classmates in other sections, casebooks for your course material other than the one assigned by your teacher. Their notes and discussions could confirm or illuminate your understanding of particular issues.

Eighth, in reviewing previous exams for the course (if those are available), consider not only how your outline would help you answer their questions but also which issues and fact patterns appear most frequently.

Ninth, when reviewing previous exams, or in general, consider: If *you* were writing the exam questions, what would you ask and why? In particular, are there any ambiguities in statutory or regulatory provisions that you've studied, or areas where caselaw has disagreed, on which you'd base at least part of an exam question?

Tenth, unless you're contributing to a group effort, your outline—including its organization, diagrams, drawings, abbreviations, symbols, index (if any), and mnemonic devices—doesn't have to work for anyone else but you. But I'll always remember some of the lessons of the contracts law professor, apparently a former DJ, who regularly referred to relevant rock music during his bar review lectures: For instance, he used Jan & Dean's *Dead Man's Curve* (1963) as an example of a counter-offer ("But I'll go you one better, if you've got the nerve. . . .").

Eleventh, preparing and then streamlining your outline might be compared to disassembling a set of Russian *matryoshka* dolls (nested, and successively smaller, figures) or to distilling increasingly concentrated forms of a solution. Although earlier version(s) might be more expansive, the final version, which to some degree you'll probably have already internalized, could be restricted to the essential points. Of course, you might well be able to use more than one version of your outline during the exam.

Twelfth, towards the end of the semester (and maybe even at regular intervals before that), you might see if a non-classmate—possibly a partner, friend, or relative—would be willing to listen to you explain at least the larger concepts of the course.

When I began teaching, as an adjunct professor at Seton Hall Law School, I quickly gained new perspectives on some of the fields in which I practiced daily. To be able to explain those subjects to students, I had to review their issues and approaches "from the ground up." Considering how to convey the most important points of a course to someone with little background in it could be an extraordinarily useful way to help you solidify your own command of the topic and to identify any aspects that you need to review.

You might add a dimension to this exercise by inviting one or two classmates to participate in your explanation. Your comments on and reactions to each other's contributions could help everyone involved. (On occasion, when I was in practice, I'd be invited to join other associates in taking out to lunch a candidate interviewing for an associate position. Some of their answers to our guests' questions taught me things about different parts of the firm.)

Thirteenth, don't assume that gaps in your outlines' coverage are your fault.

During my office hours, I've spoken with a number of students who were concerned that they couldn't find in their class notes, or in the assigned reading, answers to some of their substantive questions. Many of the students were reassured to find out not only that we'd never addressed those specific issues in class (as too advanced and/or time-consuming), but that their having identified those questions indicated that they'd probably already mastered much of the material.

Chapter 16
Effective Exam Preparation: A Semester-Long Process

Especially during your first semester, it's easy to lose track of just how much material each class has covered, and to underestimate how long it might take to review everything once classes have ended.

Probably for just that reason, the winter exams for my first year were given after the holiday break. I'm sure I wasn't the only person who, while lugging home in mid-December a duffel bag full of casebooks and class notes, appreciated having those extra days to study.

Besides starting your outline early in the semester (as discussed in Chapter 13), you might find it useful, from the very beginning of the course, to create flashcards (maybe using the index cards recommended in Chapter 11) .

Making your own flashcards enables you to capture and organize the sometimes-disconnected pieces of information you'll be receiving: for example, the geographical regions corresponding to the eleven numbered federal circuits (beyond the District of Columbia Court of Appeals and the specialized Federal Circuit Court of Appeals).

Moreover, reviewing those cards regularly, even in odd moments, can help you quickly isolate for further focus the particular items that you might find hard to remember. That could be particularly relevant if you'd otherwise be tempted to review the material simply by rereading and/or recopying it.

As noted in Chapter 1, even if you also buy commercial flashcards (which are available for the standard first-year courses), making at least some cards of your own will help you further personalize and internalize the material. Similarly, briefing your own cases and constructing your own course outlines, before comparing your results with the commercial versions, will probably give you the biggest long-term benefit.

Internalizing at least the major points of the material can be crucial even if your exam will be open book because you might not have as much time as you'd like in the exam room to consult your materials, however carefully you've annotated, highlighted, and/or tabbed them. The less you need to use your notes for anything other than details, the better off you should be.

Don't wait until the end of the semester to look carefully at previous exams for the course. As suggested in Chapter 9, you should, very early in the semester, glance through those exams, if they're available. Even before your classes build momentum, you'll be familiar with their instructions and with the format(s) of their questions, which can help you design your outline. (Also, it can be much less stressful to look at exam questions when you know that your class hasn't yet covered most of the material.)

Instead of waiting until the very end of the semester to return to those old exams, you should browse through them again at least every few weeks. You might even create a study group to discuss the ways in which you'd approach, analyze, and answer questions on material that the class has covered up to that point.

In my courses, I distribute copies of the instructions for the upcoming exam, as well as the complete exam for the previous year, well before the last class meeting of the semester, in which we review both of them. But I often get the sense that many students haven't taken advantage of the opportunity to write even outlines of draft answers before that session—perhaps because they're busy, or because they believe that "it wouldn't be a fair measurement of my knowledge, since I haven't really started studying yet."

However well you do on the exam, to help you in future semesters, after grades have been released you could read any sample or model answers that are released and attend any class meetings to review those answers. In addition, even if you were completely satisfied with your grade, you might discuss the answers individually during office hours to see if, and how, you might possibly have done even better.

Chapter 17
What to Read, After Settling In

Although you'll always have plenty of assigned reading for your courses, the following are suggestions for "extracurricular" enrichment, particularly to identify paper topics, networking opportunities, and career possibilities.

Once you're comfortable with the rhythms and patterns of the semester—or maybe during the break between semesters or during the summer after your first year—you might consider starting to spend a few minutes a day on one or more of the items below and recording, perhaps in one or more of the lists mentioned in Chapter 12, information to follow up on.

Most of the books mentioned are probably available by interlibrary loan through your law school.

First, you can easily find online different lists and categorizations (including by alphabetical order, by geographical area, and by *U.S. News & World Report* rank) of the approximately 200 accredited law schools in the United States.

Visit the Web sites of some of the schools of special interest to you or maybe in the order that they appear on part or all of one of these lists. Even if you just review the sites' home pages (which you might revisit regularly), you'll quickly notice:

- New courses, programs, centers, and other initiatives;
- New faculty members;
- Publications, activities, and other achievements of faculty members; and
- Outside speakers of special interest.

You might have to go farther into the sites to find:

- Newly formed student groups and upcoming activities of established student groups;
- Newly launched student publications and symposia or special-topic issues of established student publications; and

- Student government projects, including public interest initiatives and community and social events.

Second, you might be able to find online, or ask to have yourself added to the recipient/subscription list for digital or hard copies of, new issues of other law schools' alumni magazines.

Browsing through those publications will give you a good sense of, beyond the topics mentioned above, their faculty's latest and most interesting scholarship in a wide variety of legal fields, and maybe the "backstories" of how those authors identified and developed their topics. Also, the profiles of alumni activities, professional and personal achievements, and career trajectories could give you a better sense of your own professional possibilities and of people with whom you might discuss them.

Third, as discussed in Chapters 18 and 28, you can also find online lists of major law firms. For instance, each year the *National Law Journal* produces a "NLJ 500" list of the largest firms, ranked by their total numbers of lawyers; and (as discussed in Chapter 29) the *American Lawyer* magazine publishes its annual "AmLaw 100" and "AmLaw 200" lists of the first and second hundred firms, ranked by gross revenue.

Even if you aren't considering working for a large law firm, and even if you aren't using the most recent version of one of these lists, visiting the Web sites of some of the firms could quickly supply you with valuable insights about the firms and their current and potential clients:

- What new "practice groups" are law firms forming? (In recent years, you'd have seen announcements of the creation of ESG, blockchain, cryptocurrency, and cannabis law groups, among others.)
- Are the partners and associates in the practice groups of particular interest to you typically involved in other fields of practice as well? If so, are there common combinations of such different areas?
- Are those lawyers involved in pro bono representations or affiliated with advocacy or other associations that might be of interest to you?
- As discussed in Chapters 18 and 28, what law blogs do these sites feature (for instance, some include horse law or wine law), and what legal developments are they reporting? The beginning of Appendix F, *Topics for Papers and Blogs*, identifies 25 law firms whose sites offer particularly interesting sets of blogs.
- In what geographical areas and for what (if any) practice specialties are firms opening new offices?
- Are particular practice areas especially common among newly announced partners and/or associates?
- Are there patterns in the credentials or qualifications (such as certain types of clerkships, having worked for particular government agencies, or having earned an M.B.A. or qualified as a C.P.A.) of associates and partners in a particular field of interest to you?

Familiarity with these patterns might provide you with useful material to discuss during law firm interviews, especially (as discussed in Chapter 28) if you're ever asked for your impressions of, and suggestions for improving, the interviewing firm's site.

Fourth, as mentioned in Chapter 3, visit the American Bar Association's Web site (americanbar.org). Even if you haven't joined the group or a certain section, monitoring the topics of its sections' publications and programs and the identities of their authors and speakers can give you a good sense of what practice areas are particularly in demand and of some of their recognized experts. You might also check the bookstore section of the ABA's site for a wide variety of practice-oriented books in many different legal fields.

Fifth, for the same reasons as for the ABA's site, visit the Web sites of the bar associations of states in which you'd like to practice. Whether or not you're able to join an association and/or its sections as a student member, you might ask whether you can be added to the distribution list for the printed or digital versions of the state bar journal (another good source of items to mention during job interviews).

Sixth, check the sites of, and consider requesting that your name be added to the promotional distribution lists of, the leading legal academic publishers (such as Aspen Publishing, West/Foundation, Lexis, Carolina Academic Press, and Elgar's) for their new books, which include not just casebooks and supplements but also guides to law school and to legal writing.

Seventh, Nolo Press (nolo.com) offers the general public a large assortment of books explaining, and forms addressing, different types of legal issues (including, for example, a guide for selecting an executor of an estate, a manual for serving as an executor, and a handbook both for taking a deposition and for being deposed). They're often a good way to learn quickly about an area. In practice you might well encounter clients who have used Nolo's (or similar) forms or who have, while preparing to consult a lawyer, read some of Nolo's books.

Eighth, for their practical perspective, you might check the Web sites of legal publishers and your law school's library for books aimed at paralegals in specific areas of practice.

Ninth, the extensive and ever-expanding *For Dummies* series has produced nuts-and-bolts introductions to accounting, bookkeeping, business plans, entrepreneurship, project management, reading financial reports, probability, statistics, business succession planning, computer security, and network security, among many other topics relevant to lawyers.

One way to identify emerging trends is to periodically check Amazon's Web site for recent and upcoming additions to this series: for instance, *Social Entrepreneurship for Dummies* was published in 2010; *ESG Investing for Dummies* and *Circular Economy for Dummies* were introduced in early 2021; and *Supplier Diversity for Dummies* appeared in mid-2022.

Tenth, behind the celebrities featured on its cover page and in its first sections, *Vanity Fair* magazine often includes fascinating accounts of business controversies and scandals. The publication thus reverses the classic definition of the "mullet" hairstyle of the 1980s (perhaps best displayed by Richard Dean Anderson as television's original *MacGyver*) as, "business up front, party in the back."

Eleventh, whether or not you're interested in writing poems, short stories, poems, novels, or nonfiction articles or books, you can find many useful tips applicable to legal writing in *Writer's Digest* magazine (whose Web site also features other resources for writers).

Twelfth, in "constructing a narrative" for oral arguments or court pleadings, you might find helpful such books as: Christopher A. Booker, *The Seven Basic Plots* (2004); Ronald B. Tobias, *20 Master Plots (and How to Build Them)* (1993); and John Yorke, *Into the Woods: A Five-Act Journey Into Story* (2013).

Thirteenth, for years I've recommended that law students, lawyers, and businesspeople read some science fiction, if only to keep their minds open to new possibilities and emerging issues at the intersections of technological and cultural developments. One of the genre's giants, Frederik Pohl, reportedly said, "A good science fiction story should be able to predict not the automobile but the traffic jam."

For instance, in the 1980s and 1990s, the "cyberpunk" fiction of William Gibson and such authors as Neal Stephenson (credited with introducing, respectively, the terms "cyberspace" and "metaverse") prefigured many of the current concerns of cyberculture, -law, and -security. More recently, authors like Kim Stanley Robinson have contributed to the subgenre known as "cli-fi," which features attempts to deal with environmental emergencies and climatic crises.

If you're looking for new short stories, you might subscribe to the bimonthly magazines *Analog*, *Asimov's Science Fiction*, and/or *Fantasy & Science Fiction*.

Fourteenth, for discussions of three very useful personal and professional skills that are not always formally addressed by law schools, I recommend: Ellis Amdur, *Words of Power: A Guide for Ordinary People to Calm and De-Escalate Aggressive Individuals* (2018); Heather Platt, *The Art of Holding Space: A Practice of Love, Liberation, and Leadership* (2020); and Joe Navarro, *What Every Body Is Saying: An Ex-FBI Agent's Guide to Speed-Reading People* (2008).

Fifteenth, you might find instructive, from an agency law perspective as well as a professional perspective (Would any of his stated practices be problematic for lawyers to adopt?), the memoir, *Who is Michael Ovitz?* (2018), by the prominent Hollywood agent and co-founder of Creative Artists Agency (CAA). His severance compensation in 1996 of more than $130 million after his service of only fourteen months as president of The Walt Disney Company spawned shareholder litigation that several years later generated an influential series of Delaware court decisions on corporate governance.

Among Ovitz's observations are:

> "Sometimes, representing a client's best interests means not getting him what he thinks he wants. The judgment part of the job requires knowing when to redirect a client's desires.
>
> "I often had to offer more than I could deliver in order to be able to eventually deliver what I had offered. If the truth was bad for us, we had to change the reality, and then deliver it as what we'd said it was all along. In the meantime, well, you'd get creative.
>
> "Agencies are built on the lie that your agent will give you his total attention—but there simply isn't anywhere near enough time in the day for that."

For a revealing oral history of CAA, which features comments from Ovitz, among many others, see James Andrew Miller, *Powerhouse* (2016).

Sixteenth, as discussed in Chapter 1, you should familiarize yourself with the latest full and/or abbreviated editions of *Robert's Rules of Order*. Clients, colleagues, and adversaries might automatically adopt it, without necessarily being conversant with its intricacies, to govern various meetings, even when they might have been better served by modifying its sometimes intricate rules or creating their own customized rules of order.

The core of *Robert's Rules* appears to be a relatively manageable 220 pages of the full version: Chapter III (Sections 5-7), "Description of Motions in All Classifications"; Chapter V (Section 10), "The Main Motion"; Chapter VI (Sections 11-17), "Subsidiary Motions" (including, in Section 16, the often-misunderstood procedure to "call the question," or, in more technical terms, "move the previous question"); Chapter VII (Sections 18-22), "Privileged Motions"; Chapter VIII (Sections 23-33), "Incidental Motions" (including the dreaded "point of order"); and Section 48's discussion of the preparation, wording, and approval of minutes.

Seventeenth, browse through the "Ten-step Program to Resist Unwanted Influences" provided in six pages of *The Lucifer Effect: Understanding How Good People Turn Evil* (2007). Philip Zimbardo, a psychologist involved in the (in)famous "Stanford Prison Experiment" in 1971, two years after he pioneered tests of the controversial "broken windows theory," offers the Program as "a starter kit toward building individual resistance and communal resilience against undesirable influences and illegitimate attempts at persuasion." (The exact opposite of Groucho Marx's quip, "These are my principles. If you don't like them, I have others.")

Eighteenth, check Innsofcourt.com to see whether an Inn of Court is operating in your area and, if law students aren't eligible to be members, whether there's some way you could participate and/or assist in its operations. These professional groups regularly bring together local judges and lawyers for discussions of and presentations on legal issues and techniques, including for simulated arguments, and for mentoring, networking, and socializing. The meetings of the New Jersey Bankruptcy Inn of Court were among my most valuable professional and educational experiences when I was in practice.

Nineteenth, many years ago I read a magazine article's suggestion that to stay awake and alert during long drives, particularly at night, the driver should tune the car radio to a station that featured music or talk programs that she normally wouldn't listen to. Similarly, you might consider periodically visiting the Web sites of, if not subscribing to, publications whose political or other perspectives differ from yours, if only to expose yourself to different, though possibly unsettling, perspectives.

Finally, in his *Mastery: The Keys to Success and Long-Term Fulfillment* (1991), George Leonard, an aikido master and one of the leaders of the "human potential" movement of the 1960s and 1970s, uses analogies from the martial arts to support his argument that "[l]earning any new skill involves relatively brief spurts of progress, each of which is followed by a slight decline to a plateau somewhat higher in most cases than that which preceded it. . . . Rather than being frustrated while on the plateau, you [should] learn to appreciate and enjoy it just as much as you do the upward surges."

Chapter 18
Writing, to Be Noticed; and Nine Notes on Writing

Publishing even short articles will help demonstrate your engagement with, establish your commitment to, and develop your professional network in a specific area of law.

Whether your work is a full-length law review article, a briefer and less-footnoted analysis for a practitioners' periodical (like the magazines of state bars), or a blog post, you can find professional and personal satisfaction in the process of constructing, from many sources, your unique analysis.

Preparing an article also gives you control over a key element of your professional "portfolio," as compared to oral and written references furnished by others to your potential employers. As a writing sample for potential employers, and possibly someday as a form of marketing for clients, your work displays the power of your persuasion and prose, your ability to explain complicated subjects (especially to those—lawyers or not—without a background in the topic), your mastery of source materials, and, not least, your personal intellectual style and writing craftsmanship.

Your written work is a freestanding, stable, easily accessible (particularly if you've posted it online), and easily "portable" credential as you travel through your career.

Finally, an article can serve as your stepping-stone to creating additional materials that amplify, extend, update, and refine your analysis, and that might even ultimately affect the law and the practice of law. (Often overlooked by law students is the possibility of publishing, either as an abbreviated version of an article or paper they've written, or as a "prequel" to a much more elaborate analysis of an issue, an op-ed essay in a newspaper, particularly *The New York Times*, the *Wall Street Journal*, and *The Washington Post*, each of whose submission guidelines can be found online.)

Instead of waiting for your third year of law school to finish a "third-year paper" or "upper level writing requirement," you might consider completing it during your second year, perhaps in a paper-writing course. You would then be able to add the writing sample to your portfolio in time for third-year interviews, and you'd have the opportunity, during the intervening summer and through your final academic year, to prepare longer and/or shorter versions of, or sequels to, your work.

Your writing project will probably be more powerful and memorable if you go beyond simply describing or summarizing the state of the law, to recommend a specific approach or position. For instance:

- How, and why, should courts resolve a particular statutory ambiguity, address an emerging issue, or resolve conflicts in existing caselaw?
- How, and why, should legislators or regulators add, clarify, or delete a specific provision?
- How can companies or individual people minimize their contractual losses and/or avoid liability in certain types of transactions or interactions?

Keep in mind, of course, that your work, whether or not it's published in print or online, might resurface later in your career, particularly if you apply for positions with government agencies or for judgeships. Even if your topics and conclusions aren't controversial, they might be at odds with the positions of a potential employer or its clients.

Identifying and Developing a Topic

You might select a topic that you're already personally interested in or intrigued by, especially if looks likely to become more complex, become more relevant to potential employers and their clients, generate litigation and caselaw, and attract the attention of regulators and/or legislators.

Some issues are identified in Appendix F, *Topics for Papers and Blogs*. You might also scan the titles of panels and presentations made by the various professional groups identified after the first bullet point below, under "Enlarging Your Network. . . ."

To identify topics, you could in addition monitor Westlaw's "Topical Highlights" and Lexis's Law360 features, and ask your teachers. If you're looking for a topic of particular appeal to practitioners in big law firms, remember the saying among some practitioners that "The best clients are rich, and scared." What emerging legal issues would be particularly unsettling to, for instance, major financial institutions?

Potential employers probably assume that as a student you're comfortable with, and knowledgeable about, the latest digital technologies, devices, practices, and (sub)cultures, especially in the creation, online dissemination, and consumption of content; and also about digital assets like NFTs and payment mechanisms like cryptocurrency. These (and current elements of popular culture) may be some of the few topics on which senior partners at law firms might tend to defer to the (presumed and/or actual) experience of junior associates, or even of summer associates or interns.

You might select your topic and develop your analysis in the context of emerging social, cultural, business, technological, and demographic trends. In *Only the Paranoid Survive* (1996), Intel Corporation's former CEO and chairman Andrew Grove discussed how a company could, and should, identify and respond to "strategic inflection points," as did Columbia Business School Professor Rita McGrath, in *Seeing Around Corners* (2019).

You might also consult the tables and summaries in a recent edition of *The World Almanac and Book of Facts*. Useful for their approach, but of varying currency, are such books as Jeff Desjardins, *Signals* (2021); Rohit Bhargava, *Nonobvious* (various editions); Mark Penn, *Microtrends* (2007) and *Microtrends Squared* (2018); and Mauro F. Guillen, *2030* (2020).

Another way to find topics is to compare variations among versions of a provision in a commonly drafted document. For example, the Web sites of major corporations feature (often behind a link to "Investor Relations," "About Us," and/or "Governance") the companies' articles of incorporation (sometimes called the certificate of incorporation), their bylaws, and the charters of their standard (audit, compensation, and nomination/governance) committees.

Consider also the writing competitions to which you might submit your work once it's completed. Many such competitions are listed at lclark.edu/law/academics/student_writing_competitions/legalwritingcompetitions.blogspot.com/

Finally, don't overlook the utility of the "Frequently Bought Together" and "Products Related to This Item" displays on Amazon's product pages, which can take you down some particularly productive paths of additional books to consider. You might be able to use Amazon's "Look Within the Book" display to examine at least some of a book's specific references to certain topics, and perhaps to browse through its introduction, table of contents, and index. (That feature can sometimes be used to quickly verify quotations and page citations.)

An Early Addition to Your Résumé

As soon as you feel comfortable working with your topic, you should consider adding to your résumé, under the heading, "Work in Progress," a working title for your paper.

For this purpose, you should create a title that clearly indicates not only the nature of your topic but also that your approach and analysis will have a very practical orientation.

As an example, "Ten Factors Supporting Fee Enhancement Awards to Chapter 11 Counsel" would probably be of serious interest to law firms that represent reorganizing companies or official committees in these proceedings. Although they've almost certainly conducted their own research and listened to and read the analyses of others on obtaining a bankruptcy judge's approval of such "enhancements" (bonuses, beyond the standard, or "polestar," calculation of totaling the product of each lawyers' billing rate and her hours billed to the case) in particularly convoluted and/or novel situations, they might want to see how your conclusions compare to theirs.

By contrast, an opaque and overtly theoretical title like "Cabining and Valorizing Neoplatonic Aspects of Compensating Chapter 11 Counsel" would probably not enhance, and might well diminish, your chances of getting an interview.

Enlarging Your Network Through the Paper-Writing Process

If you're preparing your paper for a class or independent study, and the faculty member (or, if for a student law journal, your editor) agrees, you might contact, by phone or e-mail, individuals who could help you identify and refine your topic and/or approach.

Even the busiest practitioner might, at worst, merely ignore your communication. In fact, not only might such a request flatter her but she might well consider that you could someday be in a position to refer clients or matters to her, recommend her as an expert, or even give her some advice.

One way to organize this initiative would be to make a list of several potential contacts in priority order and then work down the list one name at a time, allowing two or three business days for an answer from each person before moving on to the next. You might suspend the process of contacting additional people once one has agreed to discuss an issue with you, because she might provide information that you could integrate into your questions to the next person.

You could ask anyone furnishing information to you whether she could recommend any books, articles, or Web postings and whether she could suggest anyone else whom you should contact.

Beyond members of your law school's faculty, you might approach for information or assistance about a particular issue:

- Speakers on that issue, or a related one, at programs offered by: the American Bar Association (americanbar.org); the Association of American Law Schools (AALS), each of whose many sections presents, at least once a year, a program on the latest issues in its field; the

American Bankruptcy Institute (abi.org); and continuing legal education (CLE) providers, whose programs offer updates on many different areas of law (and course credits that many states' bars require their members to earn annually), such as the Practising Law Institute (pli.edu), the American Law Institute (ali-cle.org), and state bar groups like the New Jersey Institute for Continuing Legal Education (NJICLE).

- Practitioners named in the "Best Lawyers" or "Best Young Lawyers" lists regularly published by state bars, state and city magazines, and legal organizations like the American Bankruptcy Institute (which annually produces a "40 Under 40" list). These lists could also provide examples of "career arcs," and potential sources of career advice, for your own job search.
- The authors of the blogs maintained by different practice groups at law firms, particularly those that post analyses of developments in caselaw, statutes, or regulation. The "client alerts" posted on some of these blogs might be no more than summaries of the law (designed to invite concerned current and potential clients to engage the firm to provide specific and customized advice), but even that overview could be a useful introduction to your own creative and in-depth research (which might include exploring the intersection or interaction of topics identified in two or more such updates).
- Through the relevant offices of your law school and college, their alumni who practice in or are otherwise professionally connected to the field and topic you're interested in.
- Whether or not they're affiliated with your law school, professors or other authors of law review articles or books that are particularly relevant to your topic or approach.
- One creative way to discover particularly new, and/or in-demand, areas of practice would be to contact legal recruiters (see, for instance, the Web site of the National Association of Legal Search Consultants, nalsc.org), who are retained by law firms, corporations, and other groups with positions to fill, to identify and approach potential candidates for those jobs.

  A recruiter might, considering that you could be a future prospect for one of their clients (or that you or your organization might someday become a client), share some her knowledge about the short-term and longer-term prospects for various fields of practice in different parts of the country as well as, perhaps, some tips on positioning yourself, now and later, in the job market.

A Sample Contact Message

A sample form of an e-mail to a potential source follows:

Dear ______ ,

As a [first-/second-/third-] year student at [law school name], I'm preparing a [paper/article] on [topic] for [name of class/name of journal or law review/my Upper Level Writing Requirement].

[In my discussion of (subtopic) I'm citing]
[During my research I (saw a reference to/read)]
[the article that you wrote in.../the interview that you gave to.../
the presentation that you gave to...].

I would greatly appreciate it if we could, at your convenience, briefly discuss (unrecorded),[this topic] over Zoom or by phone, which is [permitted/encouraged] by [the law school][my professor][name the journal].

In particular, I'm interested in [identify the sub-issue and perhaps one or two questions that you have about it].

Thank you for your consideration.

Sincerely,
[Name]
[phone number]

Before you send such e-mails, you should consider:

- Whether to include the e-mail address of an editor or faculty member, in case the recipient is concerned that your communication could be some form of hoax or prank.
- Whether you would agree to someone's request (or demand) to be consulted only anonymously, or perhaps with only a minimum of identification (such as, "a labor law partner at a major San Francisco law firm"). Some potential sources might not want to be identified as having contributed in any way to a paper whose conclusions they and/or their firm or clients might disagree with.
- Whether you would allow a contact (subject to any approval required by a faculty member or editor) to review any of the successive drafts of your article; and if so, whether you will permit her to make any changes to anything, such as a quotation, directly credited to her (or to insist that some or all of that information be removed from your article or that its context be revised in certain ways).

Once your article is published or posted online, you might send a copy (or link) with a note of thanks to those who assisted you (unless, as noted above, a source would not welcome even that level of recognition or documentation of her involvement).

Clearing the Publication of Your Paper

As a student intern, summer associate, or relatively new lawyer (judicial clerks might well be prohibited from publishing during—and, with regard to certain issues, even for some time after—the terms of their clerkships), before submitting articles for publication you should carefully consider whether and specifically how they will discuss the practical implications of particular legal issues and also whom in your workplace you should approach to review and approve the publication of your work.

First, an organization (not necessarily only a law firm) might consider it inappropriate for one of its employees to "give away the store" by providing detailed analyses and recommendations for free to existing or potential clients.

Second, not all of the organization's lawyers or executives might agree with your article's specific practical conclusions ("Therefore, the emerging caselaw requires clients in [Situation X] to [do Y]").

Third, an existing client might demand that the organization explain why it wasn't following or hadn't followed, in that client's own situation, specific recommendations made in your article.

Fourth, to reduce the possibility of being accused of breaching the relevant rules of professional ethics, lawyers who make their articles available, including online, to clients or potential clients, might consider adding prominent disclaimers warning that:

(1) this material does not constitute legal advice, and its receipt by the reader does not create an attorney-client relationship;
(2) the material is not guaranteed to be accurate, timely, current, or complete;
(3) the recipient should not rely on the contents of the article but instead should consult her or its lawyer for specific advice on such issues;
(4) the article reflects legal developments as of [the date of its publication], but the law may have subsequently changed; and
(5) the article does not necessarily represent the views of the employer as a whole or of any of its clients.

Some state bars also require certain e-mails or Web pages to contain, like their hard-copy equivalents, a designation such as "advertisement" or "attorney advertising."

Also of relevance in this context is one section of Formal Ethics Opinion 10-457, *Lawyer Websites*, which the ABA's Standing Committee on Ethics and Professional Responsibility issued on August 5, 2010:

> ...Lawyers may offer accurate legal information that does not materially mislead reasonable readers. To avoid misleading readers, lawyers should make sure that legal information is accurate and current and should include qualifying statements or disclaimers that "may preclude a finding that a statement is likely to create unjustified expectations or otherwise mislead a prospective client." Although no exact line can be drawn between legal information and legal advice, both the context and content of the information offered are helpful in distinguishing between the two. [footnotes omitted]

Nine Suggestions for Your Writing Process

First, immerse yourself in the material. As discussed in Chapter 12, keep track, in a digital or hard copy "research log," of what you've already read, and, for each item, what questions, issues, and sources or references it suggested to you for further inquiry. Also, you might save examples of what you consider particularly well written or organized articles or passages.

A physical or digital collection of law review articles might not be so difficult or time-consuming to go through as it might seem from their total page count, because a significant amount of the material (for example, a summary of the features of blockchain technology or of the holdings of key legal decisions) will probably be repeated by many of the articles.

Second, remember who your audience is. How much of the underlying technology or legal precedent should be emphasized because it will be new to this set of readers? How much can you assume they're familiar with?

Third, wherever possible, check the primary sources rather than relying on other sources that might have inaccurately paraphrased or summarized them, misquoted them, or quoted them out of context.

Fourth, check every direct quotation and citation as soon as you insert it into your writing.

Fifth, as you write, save in a separate hard-copy or digital file at least the portions of the sources that you've quoted so that you (and/or your editors) can double-check them. Once, to help the editors of a law review cite-check and edit the manuscript of an article in which I'd cited and quoted from many relatively rare documents, I mailed them a package containing photocopies of the title and copyright pages and pages cited or quoted of each of those sources.

Sixth, if you have the time to do so, put your work aside for a while so that you can come back later, with "fresh eyes," to proofread and polish it.

Seventh, as suggested in Chapter 12, you might construct your own customized checklist of proofreading issues, not just for standard spelling, grammar, punctuation, and citation points but perhaps also personal style issues (such as the misuse or overuse of certain words or phrases).

Eighth, if it's permitted by your course or journal, ask one or more classmates or other friends to review your drafts, not for accuracy but to see if your writing is clear enough (especially if they're not already familiar with your topic) and to catch spelling and other errors that your own proofreading might have missed.

Ninth, remember that a major corollary of the principle that "Everything takes longer than you think it will," is "Nothing writes itself."

Junior lawyers learn quickly not to take at face value even apparently sincere estimates that, "This project should only take you an hour." No matter how much research you've already organized (or been given) and how clear your outline's structure is, it's easy to underestimate how long it will take you to complete and review your work.

Another corollary: Don't count on having a sudden burst of inspiration or productivity—and an uninterrupted block of time to work—as the deadline approaches (especially since, in practice, the deadline that you were given could be suddenly and seriously shortened); instead, start early, work incrementally, and, as noted in Chapter 7, be ready at any moment to summarize your conclusions so far.

Chapter 19
Sixteen Aspects of Assessing a Law Review Article

Near the beginning of the 1989 movie, *Dead Poets Society*, the new English teacher John Keating (Robin Williams) calls on a student to read aloud to the class from the textbook's introductory essay, "Understanding Poetry."

In that passage, the (fictional) Dr. J. Evans Pritchard derives the "measure of [a poem's] greatness" by multiplying the "perfection" of its style by the "importance" of its theme. However, a disgusted Keating, insisting that, "We're not laying pipe, we're talking about poetry!", instructs the class to rip out the offending pages and deposit them in the classroom's garbage can.

Without attempting to quantify the quality of a law review article (including your own draft), you might consider the following factors in evaluating it:

First, what is the author's professional and personal background, and how might those inform (or even bias) her analysis? Does a practitioner's article seem designed to further the interests of particular clients or to defend the decisions of one or more judges before whom she frequently appears?

The initial footnote might indicate, beyond the author's institutional affiliations, any sources of funding or other support for her research, and perhaps also if she was, or is, involved in litigation or other representations connected to the article's themes.

Second, beyond her own colleagues and institution, from which academics and/or practitioners does the author, in her initial footnote, acknowledge having received assistance, support, or advice? Although not all of those individuals might agree with every facet of the published article, this list could give you some sense of the author's professional connections and community, and of her analytical orientation.

Third, how does this article fit into the author's program of scholarship? Does it update, extend, clarify, correct, and/or defend any of her previous works? Does it apply one of her previous techniques (like statistical or other empirical analysis) to a new issue? Does it introduce an idea that she promises to explore in future works? Does it borrow an approach from another author and/or field?

Fourth, for which audience(s) is the author writing? Is she trying to convince or influence law students, legal academics, lawyers, judges, legislators, and/or regulators in a particular field or fields of practice? Or a particular subgroup of any of those?

Fifth, what is the author's agenda, and why is it relevant today? Is she advocating, for example, that a certain type of legislation or legislative provision be enacted, or rescinded? That judges adopt a new method of, or consider new factors in, resolving certain legal issues? That the approaches of other commentators, or of court decisions, be modified or abandoned?

Sixth, on what sources is the author relying? Long-established—or relatively new—precedent, statutes, or regulations? Well recognized law review articles (even if only to distinguish her own work)? Legal treatises? Media reports or analyses? Documents filed with the court in litigation, submitted to a government agency, and/or posted on a corporation's Web site? Empirical data? Historical records? Personal interviews? Technological manuals? Does it seem as though these sources are complete, accurate, and relevant?

Seventh, how is the author using her sources? Is she adopting a new interpretation or method of interpreting them? Does she claim that some of the sources are unreliable, or that they have been misread or misunderstood by previous writers?

Eighth, if the analysis depends on an explanation of specific technological or other background (for example, the nature of blockchain or of cryptocurrency), do you think the author has successfully explained that topic to her intended audience(s) at the appropriate level? Does her explanation seem oversimplified or overly complex? Should the author have included a list of other sources and resources?

Ninth, what policy or other assumptions has the author made? Do they seem justified? Does she discuss how those assumptions could be tested, or the effects on her analysis if they are not entirely accurate?

Tenth, what ultimate goals does the author assert that her position will or would serve (justice? fairness? efficiency? transparency? cost-effectiveness? accountability?), and how does she define them? How much do you think that her approach would actually help the constituencies that she claims would benefit? Would these estimated overall benefits outweigh the estimated overall harms, to those constituencies and to others?

Eleventh, do you feel that the author has justified the use of her method of analysis and her conclusions? Or is the logic inconsistent, the data unreliable, or the assumptions shaky? Has she anticipated, and defended her analysis appropriately against, all such objections?

Twelfth, whether the author indicates this or not, are the conclusions of the article limited to a certain set of facts or situations, and are there any other exceptions to the application of her analysis? Do those exceptions significantly undercut her arguments?

Thirteenth, although it's not uncommon for an academic author to claim that her article is the first to address a specific issue in an "undertheorized" area, do you believe that the article actually "adds to the literature" in an important way in terms of practice and/or theory?

Fourteenth, do you think that the author wrote clearly and without unnecessary (and/or unexplained) jargon? Is her work well-organized, with a clear progression of ideas and an effective structure of sections and subsections?

Fifteenth, how does the article "flow"? Is there unnecessary repetition? Do you think that some of the material in the body of the text should have been moved to the footnotes or to an appendix, or vice versa?

Sixteenth, if the article was published some time ago, how has it been cited (if at all) by other commentators and by courts?

You might, as suggested in Chapter 14, ask a teacher during his office hours what his favorite law review articles are and why, even if those articles aren't in his fields of teaching and research and even if he doesn't necessarily agree with all of their conclusions.

My own all-time favorite law review article is (now U.S. Senator) Elizabeth Warren's compelling and extraordinarily elegant defense of the Bankruptcy Code of 1978.

In *The Untenable Case for the Repeal of Chapter 11*, 102 Yale L.J. 437 (1992), Warren, who was then a law professor at the University of Pennsylvania (and a visiting professor at Harvard Law School), responded to *The Untenable Case for Chapter 11*, which had appeared in the previous volume of *The Yale Law Journal*. That article's authors had argued, with seemingly sound statistical support, that the Code enriched corporate executives and counsel at the expense of investors and creditors.

With deceptive understatement, and even some disarming praise for the authors' attempt to apply mathematical methods to critical questions of bankruptcy policy, Warren delicately but deliberately and devastatingly disassembled their collection, sorting, and interpretation of their data.

Her article reminded me of the supposedly sympathetic Southern expression, "Bless his heart," which is not always intended the way it might sound. On another level, Warren's point-by-point rejection of the authors' empirical analysis made me think of the line by the wise but weary title character of the classic song, *The Gambler* (by Don Schlitz; released by Kenny Rogers in 1978) that if you're going to play a game, you've got to learn to play it right.

Chapter 20
Starting a Reading (or Other) Student Group

Perhaps with other interested students (and possibly under the auspices of an existing or newly created student group at your law school), you might take the initiative to found an extracurricular "reading group" on a law-related topic.

That project could not only expand and deepen the law school's formal curriculum and syllabi but enhance your own résumé and create new connections among, and networking opportunities for, you and other participants (particularly if external speakers are invited).

The administrative and logistical issues include:

- What official recognition might the group need from the law school's administration and student government?
- What funding might be available from the administration or student government; what is the process for applying for such funding; and how much, if anything, could the group initially request?
- Should membership be restricted, at least initially, to your school's law students, or opened to members of the undergraduate community and/or of other graduate schools in your university (or even to students at other graduate schools in the region)?
- Would faculty and staff be welcome to attend any or all meetings and presentations?
- How often would the group meet (for instance, monthly?), and at what time(s)?
- Would the group encourage only student presentations, only outside speakers, or a combination? (You might create a "workshop" series on a particular topic, or even a separate group involving a variety of topics, through which students could present their papers in progress for

questions, comments, and reactions by other students in a not-for-credit, non-graded, and supportive setting.)

- Would the group be able to communicate on an official law school Web page and/or using law school e-mail addresses?
- Does the school or university have any restrictions on inviting and on compensating outside speakers? Would an outside speaker need to sign any consent form for the law school or the university?
- Would any portion of the meetings—whether in-person, online, or hybrid—be recorded?
- Would the discussions be considered "off the record," or could the featured speaker, and/or other participants, be quoted? Could quotations be attributed to the speaker and/or other participants by name, or would the "Chatham House Rule" (by which statements can be quoted but not attributed to specific people) apply?
- Would students who violated a policy that prohibited recording and the dissemination of such recordings, and/or prohibited quoting participants by name, be subject to disciplinary sanctions by the law school?
- What disclaimers should the organizers provide as a matter of course (such as, "The speakers' views are not official positions of the law school") or invite the speakers to offer (for instance, that a government official is speaking in her personal capacity and not making an official statement on behalf of her office or agency)?
- What types of reading, and how much, would be selected for discussion: complete, or portions of, law review articles, books, and/or newspaper/Web site articles? Would student-authored works, whether published or in draft form, be eligible for consideration?
- Who would choose the material? A committee? An invited speaker? The vote of all members?
- How far in advance of the group meeting would the selected item(s) be identified and/or made available?
- How would the group ensure that the speakers are diverse and the discussions inclusive?
- Would the group want, or would it be required to have, an official advisor or advisory board from the faculty?
- Would the group be interested in creating an advisory board of alumni? If so, how would members of that group be selected and invited?

Among the many possible topics of such a reading group (for more, see Appendix F, *Topics for Papers and Blogs*) are:

- Training/Preparing to Be a Corporate (and/or Nonprofit) Director
- Lawyers and—and as—Leaders of Organizations

- Creative Writing (and, Possibly, Publishing) for Lawyers and Law Students
- The Lawyer's Role in Crisis Management and Media Relations
- Establishing Your Own Law Practice
- The Law of [X] [a particular industry or profession, such as: The Intelligence Community, Streaming Content Services, Music, Videogaming, Cryptocurrency, Blockchain and DeFi (Decentralized Finance), Cannabis, Psychedelic Medicine/Therapy, Autonomous Vehicles, or Large Law Firms]
- Counseling [Y] [a particular clientele, such as: Veterans, Start-Up Entrepreneurs, Start-Up Nonprofit Organizations, Social Enterprises and Social Entrepreneurs, Philanthropists, Venture Capitalists, or Social Influencers]
- The Law of Superheroes—in their Fictional Universes, and in Today's Content Industries
- Online "Creators" and the Law
- Social Influencers and the Law
- The Metaverse, for Lawyers, Law Firms, and Their Clients
- The History and Evolution of Law Schools and Legal Education

You might also create a "Law-Adjacent Speaker Series," featuring presentations by noted individuals who live and/or work in the law school's geographic area. These programs could bring to the law school community non-lawyers (or lawyers not talking about their primary professional practices) whose work creates, responds to, connects with, and perhaps invites your participation in legal issues of interest.

Such speakers might include, for example, poets, novelists, and screenwriters; reporters, columnists, and other authors of nonfiction; founders and/or leaders of nonprofit organizations; and scholars or other experts in some forms of practical ethics and equity.

Chapter 21
Of Stress, Sanctuaries, Celebrations, and Saving Worlds

We must reserve a back shop all our own, entirely free, in which to establish our real liberty and our principal retreat and solitude.
Michel de Montaigne (trans. M. Donald Frame)

In my second year of law school, after carefully reviewing the options for our single three-week "winter session" course between the fall and spring semesters, I signed up for Legal Writing.

It wasn't because I felt that I needed serious improvement in that area, but because the course was well-known to be, let us say, undemanding; and because, halfway through law school, I still had a lot of items left on my list of places to visit and things to do in Boston.

My decision appalled one of my most intense classmates (who'd once told me that he watched the stress-filled movie *The Paper Chase* "to psych myself up before exams"). He insisted, "You're cheating yourself out of the opportunity to take a substantive course!"

But I didn't doubt my choice then, and I've never regretted it since. I still remember the promising weight in my hand of the pile of T transit tokens that I bought. Over those weeks, I had a lot of fun and finally got to cross off large parts of my list.

Actually, one of the most useful things I heard in that course was the advice, "Don't think of sharpening all your pencils and straightening up your desk as procrastination—think of it as part of the writing process." I realized that taking a little time to relax in Boston was part of my law school process.

It's no revelation that law students need some sanctuaries, whether physical, virtual, or mental; whether they're solitary, or with friends or family; and whether they're part of the school's official activities (like participating in a "law revue" or talent show), unofficial groups (like a chess or running club), or (as many might recommend, for at least some of your "downtime") entirely unconnected to the law school and its community.

In one scene of *The Paper Chase*, the main character and another member of his study group decamped to a nearby hotel room as exams neared, to isolate themselves from the rising stress in the law dorms. (Another classmate told me that her parents, after seeing that movie, had offered to pay for a hotel room for her and her friends during our fall reading period.)

My own sanctuaries were sometimes simple and silent. I enjoyed long runs; and, although I regularly ate with friends in student-priced restaurants, I'd often go by myself with a used paperback novel to a Chinese restaurant that usually wasn't crowded and whose staff didn't seem to mind if customers lingered after eating.

One day, a few minutes after I finished lunch, I also finished a collection of Stephen King's short stories. In his afterword, he wrote something like, I'm not claiming that this is the world's greatest literature, but if it took you away from your day for a while and gave you a little break, then it's served its purpose. Sitting in that quiet restaurant, I thought, "That it did, Mr. King, and thank you very much."

For the same reason, right before every semester's reading period began, I'd get a few of the biggest paperback novels that I could find (often part of a series, like Frank Herbert's *Dune* or Herman Wouk's *The Winds of War*), to take study breaks with.

Only later did I discover some deeper benefits of the many hours that I'd spent browsing in the bookstores near the law school and in Boston.

First, around the time I received tenure, I started writing an article that had been inspired in part by books I'd discovered as a law student. *Owning Enlightenment: Proprietary Spirituality in the "New Age" Marketplace*, which the *Buffalo Law Review* published in 2003, examined in detail various attempts by modern spiritual groups to apply intellectual property laws to prevent the dissemination and popularization of their teachings and techniques.

Second, that project, and its spirituality-centered source materials, greatly helped me to maintain a sense of focus, control, progress, and productivity, as well as some level of normality, during the very unsettled and unsettling weeks and months following the attacks of 9/11.

Third, when a modern spiritual group contacted me about their limiting the use of their own intellectual property, I was able to contribute some practical suggestions (with the agreement that they didn't constitute legal advice).

I hope that your "outside" interests, activities, connections, and communities, whether they're online or offline, similarly support you and help you identify and explore legal issues that you find personally and professionally fulfilling.

Retaining Your Perspective

In part of your "commonplace book" (discussed in Chapter 12), or possibly in a separate document or a file folder, you might collect writings to help maintain or restore your perspective. You could include, for example, uplifting items from newspapers or blogs, song lyrics, lines from plays or movies, excerpts from spiritual and religious works, letters or cards that you received (and copies of ones you sent), and notes of things that you said, or that you heard someone say.

Of special relevance might be particularly calming or inspirational poems, which many people memorize as a mental and semi-meditative practice.

A few suggestions: William Wordsworth, *I Wandered Lonely as a Cloud*; Wallace Stevens, *The House Was Quiet and the World Was Calm*; C.F. Cavafy, *Ithaka*; Langston Hughes, *Dreams*; just about anything by Mary Oliver or by Jane Hirshfield; Max Ehrmann, *Desiderata*; Lord Byron, *She Walks in Beauty*; John Keats, *To Autumn*; Thomas Hardy, *The Darkling Thrush*; and William Butler Yeats, *The Lake Isle of Innisfree*.

Five Suggestions on Reducing Law School (and Bar) Exam Stress

I don't think there's any way to entirely eliminate exam stress, but five things that helped me might be of some use to you.

First, remember that, however the exam goes, it won't change who you are as a person.

Second, in the minutes before I began taking the New Jersey bar exam, all of the people at my table in the huge hotel ballroom were talking about how nervous we'd been. One woman said that she'd met, just minutes before, someone who'd told her that this was actually the second time he'd been scheduled to take the exam; the first time, several months earlier, he'd driven into the hotel's parking lot but hadn't been able to make himself get out of his car.

That story immediately wiped away my own worries. I thought, whatever happens today, at least I'm here, taking this exam. Let's go!

Third, during the summer that I studied for the bar I made a list of all the things that I planned to actually enjoy doing once the exam was over, especially if I could keep up the energy level that I'd been applying to bar preparation.

Fourth, like many if not most bar-preppers then and since, I realized that I was probably overstudying, but because I didn't know how much would be enough to pass, I tried to be safe rather than sorry. I signed up for an extra one-day course on bar essay-writing mostly because I didn't want to have to regret not having taken it.

In a scene in the movie *The Firm* (1993) (based on the 1991 novel by John Grisham), new associate Mitch McDeere (Tom Cruise) is summoned to a gathering of grim-faced partners who suddenly start smiling and congratulate him on having received one of the highest scores on the just-graded Tennessee bar exam. Most lawyers and law students probably thought, "What difference does that make? That guy simply overstudied."

In the context of passing the bar exam, a more appropriate approach (at least, by analogy) might be that of Dominic Toretto (Vin Diesel) in *The Fast and the Furious* (2001): "It don't matter if you win by an inch or a mile. Winning's winning."

Fifth, during the "Conquering the Stress of Law School Exams" session mentioned in Chapter 1, one of our professors passed on to us advice that he said he'd found useful as a law student: Don't study after 6:00 on the evening before an exam. He suggested that if we didn't know the material by then, we'd probably be better off just relaxing and getting some sleep.

That sounded reasonable to me, particularly during the late afternoon before the morning of my section's first exam. I walked all around the law library's reading room and study carrels, inviting my classmates to watch a movie with me.

After receiving only a series of scared stares, I went by myself. As the lights in the movie theater went down, I did wonder, for one truly terrifying moment, "What if all of those people are right, and I'm wasting valuable study time sitting here?"

I'll always be grateful to the people behind *A Soldier's Story* (starring Denzel Washington, directed and produced by Norman Jewison, and adapted by Charles Fuller from his Pulitzer Prize-winning play), because from its first moments I was completely involved in it, and I didn't worry again that night.

Two Final Notes:

First, away from the academic environment, in which exams and graduations are carefully scheduled far in advance, an appropriate time to celebrate won't always be obvious.

One of my colleagues told me that he'd once saved a vintage bottle of wine to open as soon as he'd finished the book he'd been writing. But, he said, he'd never been quite sure when that moment had arrived: When he submitted his final manuscript to the publisher? When he received the page proofs to review? When he'd returned them to the publisher? When the book was actually published? He admitted that he still hadn't opened that bottle.

I thought then, and have often thought since, about how my father would sometimes bring my mother a gift not because it was an anniversary or other special occasion, but "just because."

Every now and then, maybe you should treat someone—and/or yourself—to what my family came to call a "'just because' present."

Second, for some members of the law school community (and beyond), even more valuable than a tangible gift might be—despite our professional emphasis on verbal adroitness—a simple spoken (or e-mailed or texted) "Hello,"

"How are you?" or "Thank you," especially on a day or in a moment when they could be privately feeling particularly unrecognized, unappreciated, or unseen.

The Talmud says that "Whoever who saves a life, it is considered as if he saved an entire world." With a few kind words, or even just a nod or a smile, you might quietly, and without ever knowing it, be saving worlds.

Chapter 22
Eleven Suggestions for Answering Exam Questions

The most important piece of advice for taking exams is also the most obvious: Answer the question that you were asked (sometimes referred to as "the call of the question").

For instance, if the instructions accompanying a hypothetical fact pattern ask you to discuss whether a specific party (possibly identified as your client) is liable—or asks you, more generally, to address the legal issues as they affect that party—you should adopt that perspective in formulating your answer.

Don't be distracted by issues related to the possible liability of other parties unless they're relevant (which is not always clear-cut) to that question. If you were asked, for example, the amount that your client (A) would have to pay to another party (B), it could be relevant that A could deduct from that amount the amount of B's separate liability to A. It's also possible that, although A's liability to a third party (C) might not be relevant, you might be expected to discuss whether if A and another party (D) were jointly liable to B, A might be able to recover from D some of the amount that A paid to B.

Second, and still somewhat unsurprising: Beyond identifying the grounds that one party would have to bring an action against another and the types of relief (monetary, and/or a court's order that the other party do, or not do, something) that it might seek, you're also probably expected to analyze whether, under the caselaw, statutes, and regulations that you studied in the course, that party could actually win such a legal action.

For instance, could your client (E) successfully invoke any defenses to reduce the amount of, or eliminate, any potential liability to F? Does E have any legal grounds to argue that other parties should share in any of its liability to F?

Third, you might be expected to (or, in answering a unartfully drafted question, might need to) employ a form of conditional analysis, such as: If [X is true], then [Y] might be liable to [Z] because [H], unless [J]. If [X is not true], then [Y] might be not liable to [Z] because [K], unless [L]."

This approach might be particularly useful when the exam question is (intentionally or not) ambiguous; when the relevant contractual, statutory, or regulatory provision or the relevant passage from caselaw can be interpreted in different ways; and/or when the cases you've studied disagree with each other (another consideration while making your outline).

Fourth, be aware that some of the information that you might need to resolve an issue could have been deliberately omitted from the question. In that case, you should identify what information is missing, and indicate what difference it would make to your analysis, and possibly, where you would look for (or whom you would ask or sue) to obtain it.

In particular, although the hypothetical could be based in a mythical jurisdiction, the instructions might identify which state or federal jurisdiction's laws should govern your answer; if not, you might be at least implicitly asked to discuss the relevant laws of all jurisdictions that the course material covered and to compare and contrast their approaches.

Fifth, you might conclude that your teacher didn't sufficiently proofread the question. For example, a sentence might clearly be incomplete, or a party identified as "Alice" might seem to be the same person whom the question earlier referred to as "Adam." In such a situation, you should indicate in your answer the apparent problem with the question, then identify the assumption(s) that you're making to resolve the problem, and then proceed with your analysis.

Sixth, although it's not necessarily common, keep in mind that some of a fact pattern's information might have been deliberately included as a distraction, and that it has no relevance at all to the question you're asked to answer. You might simply ignore this material, or mention why it's not relevant. If you believe that the material was intended to misdirect or confuse you, perhaps by evoking a different situation discussed during the semester, you could take the opportunity to distinguish the two situations.

Seventh, it's probably not necessary to incorporate in your answer to a hypothetical question any free-floating generalities, political or social commentary, or (especially if there's a chance that they might be read literally) attempts at humor or sarcasm.

Eighth, you might ask your teachers whether you're expected, in answering hypothetical questions, to include a discussion of the larger themes of the course. Some might tell you that a brief discussion is fine but that you should mostly focus on analyzing the specifics of the fact pattern.

Ninth, it's probably also not necessary to use in your answer any specialized information that wasn't discussed (or at a level beyond that discussed) in class. For instance, the teacher probably isn't expecting to see in your answer material drawing on your personal experience and/or expertise in dealing with cryptocurrency. (When I write hypothetical questions, I try to avoid fact patterns that might be seen as inviting such discussions.)

Tenth, if you brought into the exam a checklist of issues and you have time after writing down a particular answer (or all of your answers), review the list quickly to see whether you might have missed one or more issues that were relevant.

Eleventh, if you're running out of time, especially if you want to correct or add to a previous answer, write at least an outline of your remaining answer(s), even if that means you're not using complete sentences.

Finally, remember that because many exams are designed to present a variety of issues and sub-issues, it's quite possible that only a few people, if anyone, will detect and fully analyze all of them. Discussing answers with other people right after the exam ends is probably not a wise idea.

Chapter 23
Considerations for Your Course Selections

Although you'll be assigned to most if not all of your first-year courses, and you might be required to take some courses (such as Professional Responsibility) during your second or third years, you'll certainly have the opportunity to choose most of your upper-level courses.

Beyond reading the law school's descriptions of the courses, talking with people who've taken them, and attending any presentations that your school offers on course selection, you could browse through the Examples and Explanations series books (possibly available in hard copy or online through your law school's library) that cover the most common courses, to get a sense of their substance.

Other general considerations, and ones that you might want to ask faculty (and possibly practitioners) about, include:

- Which courses do you think would be most useful if you have the opportunity to begin your career in your preferred area(s) of practice?
- Which courses might connect with each other in a way that interests you and supports your research, writing, and career plans?

  Even if your law school suggests or arranges "tracks" or sequences of courses for particular purposes, you could construct your own specialty/niche from a particularly creative combination of courses. As indicated in Chapter 17, you might find illustrations or inspiration in the courses and course sequences featured on the Web sites of other law schools.
- Which courses cover material for which you will be responsible on the multistate bar exam and on any bar exam(s) specific to the state(s) in which you're interested in practicing?

  Although bar review programs cover some of that material, they probably won't convey all of the subtleties and substantive depth that you'd encounter in law school courses. In addition, as their name indicates, the more you're using bar review courses to actually "review" subjects, rather than to learn them for the first time, the easier your exam preparation process should be.

- Which courses are prerequisites for (or at least have to be taken at the same time as) others? For instance, Business Associations is often a prerequisite for advanced courses in business law.

  By taking such "gateway" courses early, you not only keep your options open for later semesters, but you could be introduced to material and topics that you might appreciate more than you'd expected and might want to become more involved with.

  Some tax professors and practitioners have told me that they enjoyed their introductory tax courses so much that they felt as though they were "falling in love" with the subject. Someone who taught both environmental law and a form of commercial law often perceived as very dry said that several students in the former class were disappointed that the course was so heavily statutory (rather than focusing on "trees and bunnies"), but that many members of the other class discovered unexpectedly interesting issues and perspectives.
- Who will be teaching the course? If you particularly appreciate a certain teacher's pedagogical style and approach, she might be able to enliven subjects normally considered somewhat unexciting.
- What proportion of the courses that you plan to take in a given semester will focus mostly on the provisions of statutes or regulations?

  As I learned during a particularly demanding reading/exam period, it might not be the best idea to take at the same time a group of courses like Securities Regulation, Federal Personal Income Tax, Evidence, and Secured Transactions. Instead, you might "vary your diet" by balancing a few such heavily statute-oriented courses as those with some that focus more on caselaw or on general policy or theory.
- Will any of your courses, even if they're not officially categorized as seminars, have a relatively small number of students? Which subjects would you prefer to study in such a setting?
- If you don't take a specific course in an upcoming semester, when will it next be offered?
- If you're interested in the material of a particular course, but don't want to overload yourself intellectually during a semester, you might check with the Registrar's Office to see whether the law school's policies allow you to audit it without taking the exam or receiving a grade and/or whether you could take that course pass-fail.

  In particular, you might investigate how an audited course will be indicated, if at all, on your transcript; whether you'll be subject to the same attendance requirements as non-auditing or non–pass-fail students; whether you'll receive credit towards graduation for an audited or pass-fail course; and whether the credits for either an audited or pass-fail course count towards any limit on allowed credits for a given semester or for your entire legal education, and/or on credits beyond which you would have to pay extra tuition fees.

- You could also check, with the Registrar's Office and with the specific teacher, whether you could simply "sit in on" a course.
- If your law school is part of a university, courses offered by the undergraduate, or other graduate, units (for example, the business school) might be particularly relevant to your interests and career plans. Would the law school's and the university's Registrar's Offices allow you to take for a grade (or pass-fail), to audit, or to sit in on one or more such courses?
- To plan and optimize your exam period experience and results, consider which courses require, or offer an option, of a take-home exam over several days, rather than an in-class exam over a few hours; and consider your exam-taking preferences, especially for different types of topics. You might even be able to find the semester's exam schedule online.
- Do any courses require, or offer the option of, writing a research paper instead of taking an in-class or take-home exam?

  As discussed in Chapter 18, whether or not you can use such a course to satisfy any law school requirement of writing a "third-year paper," such a work could be a useful addition to your portfolio; and, it might be especially useful to satisfy a "third-year paper" requirement during your second year, which would not only enable you to include your work at an earlier stage of your job applications but would also give you the chance to expand on it (for print and/or online publication) during your third year.
- Which courses seem like they would be the hardest to teach yourself, particularly under time pressure, in practice?
- Similarly, in which courses will your comprehension of later material depend, as in many mathematics courses, on your mastery of earlier material in that course?

  For instance, a seminar on "Topics in Constitutional Law" might not build on itself the way that you might find in statutory courses, such as those involving the Uniform Commercial Code (Sales; Payment Systems, which is sometimes known as Negotiable Instruments; and Secured Transactions) and regulatory courses, such as Securities Regulation.
- A few months before I started law school, a *New Yorker* article by Calvin Trillin profiled the then-emerging Critical Legal Studies movement and the faculty factionalism that it had spawned at Harvard. (For a brief historical introduction to this approach, and its relation to both Critical Race Theory and "FemCrit" Critical Feminist Theory, see the online video *The Crits* (2017), by Jeannie Suk Gersen and Jackie Mow.)

Towards the end of my first year, as one of our section's professors was preparing to end a class a few minutes early, I asked him whether he had any advice for us about choosing courses.

He thought about it for only a moment before saying to us something like, "You're all aware of the ideological and cultural battles here. You should make the most of this opportunity: take courses from both sides and make up your own minds."

- Finally, take a theory course, like Law & Literature, or Jurisprudence, "just for fun," to give you some perspective on, and a different texture and taste than, your other courses.

Personally, I'd recommend that every law student, whether or not she's interested in practicing "business law" or in being a litigator, take:

- Business Associations
- Federal Personal Income Tax
- Evidence, and
- Law & Accounting.

For students focusing on business law, I'd add:

- Corporate Bankruptcy
- Corporate and Partnership Tax
- Corporate Governance
- Securities Regulation
- Business Planning, and
- Either or both of Negotiable Instruments/Payment Systems and Secured Transactions.

Chapter 24
Five Surprising Secrets of Business Law

In the summer during which my judicial clerkship ended, a middle-aged acquaintance of my parents asked me where I'd be working in the fall. I was proud to be able to tell her that I'd be joining the corporate department of one of New Jersey's largest law firms.

But, without a trace of a smile, she immediately said, "So, you're selling out, huh?"

I can't remember exactly what my (polite) answer was, after I'd realized that she wasn't joking.

Every semester that I teach Business Associations (which involves agency, partnership, limited liability company, and corporate law), I begin the course with that story. Even if only a few people might really need to hear it, I want to reassure everyone in the course that studying and practicing business law won't automatically compromise their personal and professional morality and integrity. In fact, I believe that the opposite has never been more true: The study of business law has never been more compatible with, and relevant to, issues of human rights, social justice, fairness, and legal ethics.

When I was a second-year law student, a Law & Economics professor, after drawing several supply-and-demand curves and calculations on the blackboard, came to some conclusion that so offended me that I didn't even raise my hand before objecting, "But that's not fair!"

Which mostly seemed to amuse him. Very calmly, he said, "Fairness doesn't have anything to do with it."

I had a very hard time paying attention to the rest of that course. I thought, and still believe, that trying to find fairness (although definitions of that concept can certainly diverge) has everything to do with legal practice.

Despite some students' suspicions that enrolling in Business Associations might be their first step on the road to becoming a soulless corporate drone, the inescapable moral dimensions of the subject can make the course one of the most morality-oriented in a law school's entire curriculum.

In fact, Business Associations—and to some degree, the study of business law in general—might surprise you in at least four other ways.

Second, the course involves very few hard numbers (other than those relating to deadlines for taking certain actions or to the proportions of votes required for a proposal to be approved by a company's owners or managers). Reflecting the difficulty of designing "one-size-fits-all" answers for the possible permutations of parties and positions, often the statutes, caselaw, and privately adopted rules (such as a company's partnership agreement or bylaws) are neither precise or pristine, but instead flexible and accommodating.

For instance, courts have created lists of factors to be applied in reviewing certain business-related decisions, and academic articles have attempted to statistically evaluate the ways in which those factors have been employed in different circumstances. Corporations are careful to characterize their own posted "governance principles" as—just as the Pirates' Code was described in *Pirates of the Caribbean* (2003)—"more what you'd call guidelines than actual rules."

Third, despite what many people—and even many lawyers—believe, corporate law doesn't require boards of directors to make every decision to maximize value for shareholders, at least in the "short term" (which itself is an imprecise concept). The corporate laws of most states specifically allow directors to consider the interests of such non-shareholder "stakeholders" as the company's customers, employees, and suppliers, and the residents of the areas in which the company's facilities are located.

In fact, as discussed in Chapter 25, one of the most exciting and quickly evolving areas of practice—and one that many law firms have created special practice groups and law schools have launched programs to address—involves Environmental, Social, and Governance (ESG) issues, that is, the ways in which companies can be responsive and responsible not only to their shareholders but also to their other stakeholders. Reversing generations of corporate reticence, corporations and their chief executive officers are now taking, and are increasingly expected by the public and their own employees to announce, positions on political, social, and cultural issues.

Fourth, most states' laws also allow qualifying corporations to identify themselves as "benefit corporations" or as a similarly designated form of "social enterprise." Neither non-profit companies (for tax purposes) nor traditional for-profit companies, social enterprises are designed both to make some (if not the maximum) profit and to satisfy one or more identified social goals.

As an alternative, or in addition, to meeting the statutory requirements of a social enterprise, a company may apply to an independent third party such as B Lab (bcorporation.net) to be certified as a "B Corporation," which has pledged to pursue, and is making progress towards, one or more social goals. For an especially informed discussion of this topic, see Christopher Marquis' book, *Better Business: How the B Corp Movement is Remaking Capitalism* (2020).

Fifth, many students may not have fully considered the extent to which the issues of the Business Associations course are integral to their daily lives, as well as to their professional opportunities.

With the high-profile collapses of companies like Enron (2001) and WorldCom (2002), regulators began to scrutinize the role and responsibilities of directors. More recently, the increased economic, political, and cultural involvement and the pervasive influence of technology companies like Apple, Facebook (now Meta), Google (now Alphabet), Amazon, Twitter, and Netflix have truly made their own governance structures and practices a matter of "everyone's business."

Many employers, clients, and adversaries are themselves organized as (or employed by) a form of partnership, corporation, or limited liability company, and even "non-business" lawyers like those engaged in family law will deal with issues involving the division or inheritance of family businesses, or with individual clients or adversaries who are partners, directors, or officers in different companies.

Not only are mainstream religious organizations like the Catholic Church organized in corporate form (in recent years, a number of dioceses and archdioceses have declared bankruptcy) but so are organizations that might seem countercultural and even otherworldly.

For example, in March 2010, an *Atlantic* magazine article, *Management Secrets of the Grateful Dead*, reported that the band "incorporated early on, and established a board of directors (with a rotating CEO position) consisting of the band, road crew, and other members of the Dead organization."

In addition, Thomas Dowling's thought-provoking book, *Shoes Outside the Door: Desire, Devotion, and Excess at San Francisco Zen Center* (2002), chronicles the corporate and cultural crisis that led to a governance overhaul at one of the country's most prominent communities of Zen practitioners. One member of the Center told Dowling, "Some of us were slow to think in those terms. We thought we were outside the world of corporate life." (For a discussion of a different Zen center's response to another type of emergency, see Appendix G, *Zen and the Art of Crisis Management*.)

Moreover, law students will find that their training in the basic principles of business associations supports their candidacies for positions as, and their service as, not only leaders of student groups but also directors of for-profit companies or non-profit organizations. See, for example, the issues outlined in Appendix E, *Policies, Procedures, and Practices for Decision-Making by Voting* (also referred to in Chapter 15).

Finally, a background in business law will help students evaluate investment opportunities for themselves and others, whether in start-up companies, publicly traded corporations, or pension funds, or in the ownership of a unit in, and participation in the governance of, a housing cooperative or condominium association.

Appendix H includes *Creative Career Suggestions for ESG and Corporate Law* and concludes with a list of organizations dedicated to promoting the diversity of boards of directors.

Chapter 25
ESG Law, Practice, and Resources

Environmental, Social, and Governance (ESG) law encompasses a quickly evolving range of issues not only across the law school curriculum but also spanning various practice areas of law firms, including environmental, corporate, securities, labor/employment, and human rights law and approaches to crisis management (sometimes referred to as minimizing a company's "reputational risk").

ESG practitioners attempt to help companies balance the monetary interests of their shareholders with the sometimes-conflicting concerns of such non-shareholder stakeholders as the company's employees, customers, and suppliers and the residents of areas in which the company operates.

Many of these lawyers probably didn't aim directly towards working in this area, even when it began to be known, years ago, as "Corporate Social Responsibility." But today's law students might find ESG law to be one of the most personally, as well as professionally, fulfilling fields of practice, and one which, by its multifaceted nature, should be especially welcoming to participants from a variety of backgrounds and perspectives.

Among the concerns of ESG lawyers are:

- How will the company prioritize (if not always harmonize) the possibly conflicting concerns of its stakeholder constituencies?
- If a company is not legally required to conform to a specific standard for a goal like sustainability or workplace diversity, how does it choose which existing standard to adopt, or define its own standard?
- To what degree are recognized standards, some of which are global rather than domestic, themselves changing or likely to change?

- How will the company measure its progress on different ESG initiatives and towards various ESG goals?
- How, and with what involvement by in-house and outside counsel, will the company collect information on its progress and report such progress to shareholders?
- Are such reports subject to the same legal standards of accuracy as are the company's financial reports? Even if they aren't, how can the company best avoid accusations of "greenwashing"?
- Under what circumstances can the company, its executives, and its counsel be held personally liable for inaccuracies in those reports?
- How will the company identify emerging ESG issues, and which elements of its governance architecture (the full board? a standing or special committee of the board? a task force or working group of directors and senior officers?) will develop proposals to address it?
- Should the company create the position of a Chief Sustainability Officer (CSO)? A Chief ESG Officer? Should the company consider for any of those positions only candidates who are lawyers? How does the role and responsibility of someone in such a position relate to that of the company's in-house General Counsel?
- What are the "best practices" for ESG, whether in a company's particular industry or generally?
- What ESG practices should a company require its suppliers (and its outside counsel) to adhere to—for instance, with regard to human rights of their employees? What practices should a company adopt at the request (or insistence) of its suppliers and/or customers?
- To what degree should an executive consider herself constrained by her fiduciary duties to the company to refrain from engaging even in entirely legal activities—including publicly stating her personal views on issues of corporate and/or social concern—if that conduct is, or could be seen as, inconsistent with any of the company's ESG initiatives?
- How should a company's ESG initiatives be revisited if it becomes financially troubled and if it files for a Chapter 11 reorganization? Are its ESG commitments, by their specific terms and/or by industry (if not public) expectations, legally binding obligations? If not, can a company reduce or eliminate them "until we get back on our feet, financially"? Alternatively, could a company in or approaching insolvency or bankruptcy legitimately adopt new or more aggressive ESG plans as a strategy to raise its reputation and resuscitate its fortunes?

Students interested in becoming more informed about, writing about, and perhaps practicing in, "the ESG space" might find of particular interest four sets of materials, not only as sources for papers but also as examples of a variety of drafting techniques:

First, the actual (and, often, annual) reports (sometimes called Sustainability Reports, or Social Responsibility Reports) that major corporations have added to their Web sites to indicate the range and extent of their initiatives in this area.

Second, the "No Action Letters" database available on the Securities and Exchange Commission's Web site (sec.gov) and on the proprietary Westlaw and Lexis-Nexis services. A board of directors can explain in detail to the SEC why one or more of the applicable regulatory provisions should allow it to omit a shareholder proposal (which it usually includes in its application) from the voting agenda at an upcoming meeting of shareholders, and can request official assurance that the exclusion wouldn't trigger an SEC action against the company. The original proposal, the company's application, and the SEC's response and reasoning can be of great interest to the governance community.

Third, decisions from Delaware's Court of Chancery (its specialized corporate court), and from the state's Supreme Court, concerning the interpretation and application of Section 220 of the Delaware General Corporation Law (DGCL), which governs shareholders' rights to inspect corporate documents.

Boards' attempts to limit the disclosure of corporate information to shareholders—and to restrict the uses or further dissemination of information that is disclosed to some shareholders—have generated hundreds of detailed and fact-sensitive decisions, and this intersection of corporate, ESG, and litigation practice should remain popular (and a topic for productive and practical legal blogging) for the foreseeable future.

Fourth, the guidelines and policy statements of leading: asset management firms (BlackRock, State Street, and Vanguard); pension funds (California Public Employees' Retirement System (CalPERS), California State Teachers Retirement System (CalSTRS), and Teachers Insurance and Annuity Association (TIAA)); and proxy advisors (ISS and Glass Lewis). The degree to which investment funds can legally encourage, or require, companies to adopt particular ESG initiatives—at the possible loss of potential profits for the companies' and the funds' own investors—is a question of increasing concern to commentators and legislators.

Chapter 26
Compliance: A Corporate, Cultural, and Curricular Crossroads

Corporate compliance—helping a board of directors design, install, implement, and monitor company-wide policies, systems, and mechanisms to prevent and detect violations of applicable laws and regulations—is a quickly growing field for lawyers and an extraordinary opportunity for law students to combine courses from several areas in a concentration (for instance, health care compliance) that meets their own interests.

The federal Organizational Sentencing Guidelines, formulated in 1991, take into account, in reducing a corporation's "culpability score" (and thus its punishment) for the criminal actions of its agents, "[the efforts made by the corporation] prior to the offense to prevent and detect criminal conduct, the level and the extent of involvement in or tolerance of the offense by certain personnel, and the organization's actions after an offense has been committed."

Particularly helpful to a corporation in this context would be for it to have adopted "an effective compliance and ethics program" to "promote an organizational culture that encourages ethical conduct and a commitment to compliance with the law."

First created by corporations on a large scale in the early 1960s, compliance programs have been developed in response to scandals involving antitrust prosecutions, illegal campaign contributions, kickbacks, bribes to foreign officials, insider trading, and fraud. More recent compliance concerns include product liability and cybersecurity.

These programs address not only the obligation of a company's agents to adhere to federal and state regulations specific to its industry (for instance, in such fields as banking and health care, or those with particular environmental issues), but also more generic corporate concerns, such as sexual harassment policies, confidentiality policies, and the Foreign Corrupt Practices Act's (FCPA) prohibitions of bribery.

The U.S. Department of Justice Criminal Division's "Evaluation of Corporate Compliance Programs" memo, as updated in June 2020, directs prosecutors of a law-violating company to consider, among other "fundamental questions," the "Commitment by Senior and Middle Management" to its compliance program.

That is, "What compliance expertise has been available on the board of directors? Have the board of directors and/or external auditors held executive or private sessions with the compliance and control functions? What types of information have the board of directors and senior management examined in their exercise of oversight in the area in which the misconduct occurred?"

Some boards have created compliance committees to oversee the company's adherence to federal and state statutes and regulations and to the company's own internal ethics and conduct codes; to educate the board and employees about those requirements; and to develop and implement a compliance program, including compliance reporting.

The recently added position of chief compliance officer (CCO) at many companies has raised questions including: Should the CCO report to the compliance committee, to the CEO, to the general counsel, or to the board? Should the company require that its CCO be a lawyer? Should a company's chief legal officer (CLO) or general counsel also serve as its CCO?

Many large law firms include, among the capabilities of their corporate (or corporate governance, or compliance) practice groups, internal investigations (often led by partners with prosecutorial and/or regulatory enforcement experience); some have formed special practice groups for this purpose. Very useful examples of, discussions of, and recommendations for improving compliance and governance (as well as examples of a specialized style of drafting) can be found in internal investigation reports that have been made publicly available by boards.

Easily available online are reports including:

- Independent Directors of the Board of Wells Fargo & Company, Sales Practices Investigation Report (2017)
- Covington Recommendations for Uber (2017) [sometimes referred to as "the Holder Report"], and
- Report to the Board of Directors of General Motors Company Regarding Ignition Switch Recalls (2014) [sometimes referred to as "the Valukas Report"].

Chapter 27
Fourteen Advantages of Studying and Practicing Bankruptcy Law

For many reasons, law students might consider studying and practicing personal or corporate bankruptcy law.

First, each of these ever-evolving legal fields is complex enough to form a specialty of its own, not just for individual lawyers but for practice groups and even entire "boutique" law firms.

In his nonfiction book *A Feast for Lawyers: Inside Chapter 11- An Exposé* (1989), novelist Sol Stein recounted his frustrations and anger during the bankruptcy of his publishing company. He observed, "The chances are that whatever lawyer a businessman usually relies on for advice will have to pass that executive on to a specialist in bankruptcy law who is willing to handle a debtor. . . . [M]any of the attorneys who specialize in this field are a breed unto themselves."

As Stein recognized, many bankruptcy specialists, whether in personal or in corporate bankruptcy, might further focus on representing primarily debtors or instead on representing personal and corporate creditors (including financial institutions) to whom the debtors owe money.

Second, because the primary statute involved is federal—the Bankruptcy Code of 1978 (Title 11 of the United States Code)—a lawyer's bankruptcy expertise might be more easily "portable" than a state-law-centered practice if she chooses to relocate to another jurisdiction.

Third, because of the intricacies of their practice, members of the bankruptcy bar in any jurisdiction are likely to form a relatively close-knit professional community, and each jurisdiction will develop and modify its own, uncodified, "local bankruptcy culture." Stein described the corporate bankruptcy bar in New York as "a smallish clan whose members work with each other in case after case," and noted that clients "can't go too far afield to find someone because you need a lawyer who's had some experience in the court that has jurisdiction."

Fourth, although bankruptcy law might be most obviously useful in troubled economic times (in an episode during the 2011-2012 season of the television series *The Good Wife*, a senior partner at a fictional law firm declared that, "If there's one department that will survive a double-dip recession, it's bankruptcy!"), even in better circumstances it's essential for helping clients anticipate and minimize commercial damages from their own or another party's potential insolvency or bankruptcy.

Fifth, like the federal Tax Code, the Bankruptcy Code attempts to balance, if not completely harmonize, often-conflicting choices in social policy and the interests of different constituencies (including different types of creditors). That balance applies not only in a person's or company's liquidation of debt (through the Code's Chapter 7, under which a corporation would cease to operate) but also in a person's or company's attempt to reorganize its debt through a repayment plan (through Chapter 11 for companies, which would be allowed to continue to operate if enough creditors, and the court, approve their "plan of reorganization"; and Chapter 13, for individuals).

Sixth, the corporate bankruptcy system is, in many situations, the ultimate arena for resolving liability and obtaining payment for serious harms, including those caused by defective products (such as some breast implants and contraceptive devices) and sexual abuse (by, for instance, some agents of the Boy Scouts of America or of the Catholic Church). For a critical account of one of the country's most recent high-profile bankruptcies, written by an activist who, though not a lawyer, served as co-chair of the reorganization's official committee of unsecured creditors, see Ryan Hampton's *Unsettled: How the Purdue Pharma Bankruptcy Failed the Victims of the American Overdose Crisis* (2021).

Seventh, corporate bankruptcy law touches many other areas of law, depending on the nature of the debtor's business, so a bankruptcy lawyer would be connected to, and add a dimension to, many different practice groups at a law firm. For reports on the bankruptcy proceedings of two very different types of companies, see Dan Raviv, *Comic Wars: How Two Tycoons Battled Over the Marvel Comics Empire—and Both Lost* (2002) and the much more technical account by Sujeet Indap & Max Frumes, *The Caesars Palace Coup: How a Billionaire Brawl Over the Famous Casino Exposed the Power and Greed of Wall Street* (2021).

Eighth, the Bankruptcy Code doesn't define many of its own key terms and critical concepts, leaving courts to develop sometimes differing definitions and multi-factor tests to fill these gaps. Bankruptcy lawyers, and those interested in writing or blogging about these legal issues, face no shortage of exciting and very practical topics to address. For instance, among the most recent issues is the treatment in bankruptcy of such digital assets as cryptocurrency and NFTs.

Ninth, like the Tax Code, the Bankruptcy Code—which in 1979 replaced the Bankruptcy Act of 1898, and which was significantly amended and updated in 1984, 1994, and 2005—is the subject of continual proposals for its further revision.

Tenth, as counsel for a debtor or creditor, you might be able to help people (including executives) through situations of great personal stress. Sol Stein probably found some form of comfort and perspective in writing his book; but in it, he recalled having spoken with deeply depressed owners of other companies in bankruptcy.

Eleventh, on a related note, the policy and practice issues of personal or corporate bankruptcy law raise such major political and cultural themes as:

- Punishment vs. rehabilitation
- Optimism vs. realism
- Shame and redemption
- Federal vs. state law
- Monitoring, enforcement, and compliance (not only of debtors but also of creditors)
- The lawyer's involvement in legal rather than business decisions and her ability to distinguish between them
- The degree to which a lawyer should know, or learn, the details of a particular client's business or industry
- Special questions of legal ethics (especially with regard to conflicts of interest) and of preventing and not facilitating a client's bankruptcy-related crimes (such as concealing a debtor's assets from the court)
- Concerns about controlling precedent (because of the sometimes confusing appellate system in bankruptcy law)
- Methods of statutory interpretation
- Definitions, and metrics, of "success," "efficiency," and "fairness," and
- Scalability (Do the same laws and principles apply to all personal or corporate debtors? Or are some "too big to fail"?)

Twelfth, because of the numerical data submitted by debtors in their bankruptcy petitions, this area of law is extremely susceptible to empirical analysis. (See the discussion at the end of Chapter 19.)

In fact, about twenty-three years before she became a United States Senator, Professor Elizabeth Warren (then at the University of Pennsylvania Law School) co-authored the groundbreaking book, *As We Forgive Our Debtors: Bankruptcy and Consumer Credit in America* (1989), which concluded from a statistical evaluation of personal bankruptcy petitions that such debtors, far from abusing the bankruptcy option, were not only generally in severe financial distress but, in many cases, would have been better-served by filing much earlier than they actually had.

(One surprising fact about the Bankruptcy Code is that it does not directly address the extent to which a company has to be experiencing—or anticipating—financial hardship, in order to be eligible to file for bankruptcy. This is one of the many bankruptcy issues for which different courts have developed their own multi-factor tests.)

Thirteenth, particularly in high-profile bankruptcy cases, you might well be able to find the courts' dockets online and to download for free all of the parties' court filings. Instead of simply reviewing media summaries of developments, you can read the original documents and not only learn what popular reports are omitting (or getting wrong) but also get a sense of the lawyers' drafting styles and craftsmanship, as well as of many possible topics for papers or blogging.

Fourteenth, taking one or more bankruptcy courses will support your application for a clerkship not only with a bankruptcy court, which would be an extraordinarily valuable year of education in this area's intricacies (and would position you well to join a firm's bankruptcy practice group), but also with federal district courts (which technically "refer" jurisdiction over these matters to the bankruptcy courts) and Courts of Appeals, to which bankruptcy issues can be appealed.

You might be interested in the extremely useful *The Attorney's Handbook on Consumer Bankruptcy and Chapter 13* and *The Attorney's Handbook on Small Business Reorganization Under Chapter 11*, both of which are published by Argyle Press.

For a very practical discussion of consumer bankruptcy, I also recommend Cara O'Neill's books (from Nolo Press) for the layperson, *How to File for Chapter 7 Bankruptcy* and *Chapter 13 Bankruptcy: Keep Your Property & Repay Debts Over Time*.

Chapter 28
Preparing for, and Succeeding During, Job Interviews

In preparing for a job interview with a law firm, beyond reviewing its Web site and the site's pages for your potential interviewers, you might check the Westlaw and/or Lexis databases for recent state or federal decisions in which members of the firm were identified as counsel to one of the parties (and, possibly, for actions brought by or against the law firm itself).

You might even (perhaps with the assistance of the law library's reference staff) locate online the dockets for high-profile bankruptcy and other litigation in which the firm's lawyers have appeared on behalf of one of the parties, and browse through some of the firm's recently filed pleadings.

Whether or not you're applying for a position in business law, or even at a large law firm—and whether or not you agree with the *Wall Street Journal*'s editorial positions—reading that newspaper daily (possibly online for free, through your law school's library) for a week before (and especially on the morning of) an interview could provide you with useful items to bring up, especially regarding business, technological, and cultural trends.

You might also consider browsing, for at least a few days before the interview, a Web site of a major local newspaper covering the city or state of the office that you're applying for a position in (if the firm has several offices).

Also, the day before, if not that morning, check online for developments in the areas of law that you'll be interviewing about and on the issues addressed by your writing sample (which you should re-read a day or two before the interview, and which you could take extra copies of, with your résumé, to the interview). For instance, if you're applying for a position in corporate law, you could visit the Web sites of the Delaware Court of Chancery and the Delaware Supreme Court, on which decisions are posted the same day that they're issued.

Reading Recent Relevant Books

You might also find it useful to read at least one recent nonfiction book concerning the type of law that you might be practicing and/or prominent companies and individuals in the relevant industries.

For example, students applying for a business law position involving high technology and/or intellectual property might consider one or more of: Mark Bergen, *Like, Comment, Subscribe: Inside YouTube's Chaotic Rise to World Domination* (2022); Tripp Mickle, *After Steve: How Apple Became a Trillion Dollar Company and Lost Its Soul* (2022); Jimmy Soni, *The Founders: The Story of PayPal and the Entrepreneurs That Shaped Silicon Valley* (2022); Dade Hayes & Dawn Chmielewski, *Binge Times: Inside Hollywood's Furious Billion-Dollar Battle to Take Down Netflix* (2022); James Andrew Miller, *Tinderbox: HBO's Ruthless Pursuit of New Frontiers* (2021); and Tim Higgins, *Power Play: Tesla, Elon Musk, and the Bet of the Century* (2021).

Each of those books chronicles a string of very successful strategies and decision-making by a major company's executives (and, to a lesser degree, by its counsel); but each also underscores the importance of the company's remaining extremely sensitive to and adapting to (and, maybe, sometimes leading) changes or potential changes in its market.

You might even read a few treatments of the same subject so that you can compare and contrast them. For instance, less than admiring accounts of Juul and other producers of e-cigarettes and vaping products include Lauren Etter, *The Devil's Playbook* (2021) and Jamie Ducharme, *Big Vape* (2021); and, of Adam Neumann and his former company, WeWork, Eliot Brown & Maureen Farrell, *The Cult of We* (2021) and Reeves Wiedeman, *Billion Dollar Loser* (2020).

A week or so before the interview, you could check online for reviews of the book(s) you've chosen and also for updates on the company's evolution since the events discussed.

In some cases, you might want to have read a book that came out only days or weeks before your interview, to convey some sense of your enthusiasm for and engagement with the area. That could be especially helpful if your interviewer hasn't read the book himself and might be interested in hearing your summary of various points and your reaction to its reviews in mainstream media.

You might be prepared to discuss with the interviewer:

- How well written did you think the book was?
- What would you have liked to see the author provide (or provide more) information on or analysis of?
- What parts of the book surprised you?
- What actions, by the company and/or some of its executives and counsel, most impressed you?
- What actions did you most disagree with?
- What would you recommend that the company do today?

- What larger lessons did you take from the book, for other companies, for businesspeople, and their lawyers?

Faculty members should be able to recommend to you relevant books from their areas of scholarship and teaching. Also, the *Wall Street Journal*'s daily book review often focuses on books useful for this purpose.

Stereotypes that may well work in your favor are that law students might, as summer associates or first-year associates, display more energy, enthusiasm, tech-savviness, and, possibly, exposure to cutting-edge legal doctrines than many more senior associates.

You might also be prepared to discuss a novel (or fiction series), whether or not it's recent or law-related, in case you're asked, "Have you read anything good for fun lately?"

Also, if you've listed a particular interest on your résumé, consider what books about it you might recommend should an interviewer ask (whether from sincere curiosity or as a test of your familiarity with the area).

Dining Issues

If you're being interviewed over a meal, remember the stories about employers who immediately ruled out a candidate who put salt on her food before tasting it.

When I was in practice, I had an interview over lunch with a senior partner at a private club. When the waiter served me the wrong dish, I politely repeated what I'd ordered, and minutes later the waiter returned with it.

I've often wondered whether that was the partner's prearranged test, to see whether, for the sake of politeness or maybe because I wasn't paying attention, I'd just eat the wrong food; or to see whether I'd say something inappropriate to, or about, the waiter.

For years, I also thought that this very suspicion might be somewhat excessive, but then I read a *New York Times* interview in which a senior executive mentioned that he'd used exactly that strategy when interviewing job candidates.

Vibes

If you assume that the employer chose your interviewer as one of the more impressive and personable—or at least, as a typical—member of the employer's legal group, how do you feel about him or her? What do you think that says about the employer?

It's not exactly the same thing, but when I was applying to colleges, I had an interview with a local alumnus of MIT. When I asked him whether MIT offered courses in Latin, which I was then studying at an advanced level, he literally sneered and then told me that at MIT I could probably get credit for any Latin courses that I took at a nearby university. I suddenly started wondering how I'd feel if, at MIT, I decided not to major in math or science; and I never completed my application.

If the interview's held in the employer's office(s), pay attention to how you feel about the environment, on a gut level.

Once, a student who'd received offers from two big law firms asked for my advice on choosing between them. He'd prepared a detailed list comparing the firms in various ways, but after a minute of reading aloud from it he looked up and said, "You know, at one of the firms people were friendly and smiling and laughing, and at the other one everyone just seemed very serious"; and then he dived back into the list. "Wait," I said, "didn't you just mention a difference at least as important as the ones you wrote down?"

Asking Questions

You should be prepared to ask the interviewer a few thoughtful questions. Your law school's career development office will surely have detailed advice and examples for this, but among the questions I'd recommend are:

- What type of training do associates receive in [a particular practice group or area of interest to you]?
- What role, if any, do associates have in marketing and client development?
- [However much you might actually like, or even prefer, research and analysis,] Do junior associates have many opportunities for client contact?
- What do you personally consider the best (or most interesting, or most rewarding) part(s) of your work?
- What Web sites, books, or periodicals do you recommend that I read to learn more about and to keep up in your area(s) of practice?
- What resources do you suggest that I *not* read (because they're outdated, inaccurate, or biased)?

The Employer's Web Site

You might also refer to material on the employer's blog(s), especially if it was posted by your interviewer(s), although an interviewer might be neither involved in nor interested in blogging (and might believe it to be a waste of otherwise billable time).

If (as discussed in Chapter 17) you've been monitoring the employer's Web site for some time and have noticed significant changes in its appearance and/or content, you might want to mention those.

Be prepared, if asked, to offer a few constructive suggestions about how the blog(s) or the Web site might be enhanced, especially if you're familiar with the sites of the employers' competitors. However, this could be tricky if there have already been disagreements within the firm about some of the issues you identify.

For instance, here are three concerns that are not mere questions of aesthetics but actually involve questions of a law firm's professional ethics:

First, in order to avoid accusations that they disclosed confidential material, and to prevent themselves from having to resign from the representation of an existing client because they received information that an opposing party expected to remain confidential, some law firms design their lawyers' pages to display a click-through message when a visitor clicks on a lawyer's e-mail address. The message warns that no attorney-client relationship exists, and no confidential details should be sent, until the firm agrees that it can take on the potential representation.

However, if that lawyer's address (for example, Jane.Doe@LawFirm.com) is already displayed on the site (or if, when the visitor's cursor is over the link, the address becomes visible at the lower left corner of the screen), there's no guarantee that a visitor to the Web site will use that link and be forced to see that disclaimer; he might just type the address into his separate e-mail program.

Second, even firms whose lawyers' links don't indicate their e-mail addresses sometimes have a pop-up, "click-through" disclaimer that indicates, or suggests, that the restriction on sending confidential information without prior approval doesn't apply to existing clients. Technically, it would be far safer for the firm to state explicitly that even an existing client with a new legal matter should heed this warning, because the new situation might itself involve a conflict.

Third (as discussed in the "Clearing the Publication of Your Paper" section of Chapter 18), if law firms publicly post articles and other legal analyses prepared by their lawyers, it's probably preferable to indicate conspicuously, whether by a click-through box or in a notice next to the article (rather than in a "terms and conditions" page for the entire Web site), the date that the material was produced, a disclaimer that it might no longer be accurate, and a general disclaimer that it does not constitute legal advice.

Terms and Conditions

Remember that, for all the talk that you might hear about "teams" at the firm, there will almost certainly still be a hierarchy, with newly graduated lawyers near the bottom.

Also, although it's probably not something you should ask about (because it could make you look less than fully committed to working hard), any "average billable hours" or "expected billable hours" figure supplied by the firm or your interviewer could be misleading in at least three ways.

First, an associate who wants to distinguish herself will probably want to accumulate significantly more billable hours than the "official" or required average.

Second, many activities, such as training, client development, or administrative activities for the firm, might not be considered part of your billable total; nor, of course, are the firm's social events.

Third, some firms might not count towards your total billable hours all of the time that you actually spent on substantive work for a client, if they, recognizing the natural inefficiencies of even very talented junior lawyers, reduce that time to a more "reasonable" amount before billing the client.

For these reasons, a goal of (for example) 2,000 billable hours might seem misleadingly simple to reach. A law student might calculate: If I took a two-week vacation, I'd work fifty weeks per year, so to reach 2,000 hours over fifty weeks I'd need to bill forty hours per week. If I don't work on weekends (stop laughing, you lawyers), I'd have to work eight hours every weekday. So, if I start working at 9:00 every weekday morning, and take an hour for lunch, I can stop working at 6:00 every weekday evening.

That is not how it works.

That is not how you will find yourself working.

Chapter 29
Seven Books About Large Law Firms

When I was in practice, I quickly lost count of how many times veteran lawyers told me, wistfully, some version of, "Law once was a profession—and now it's just a business."

Even then, I never believed them. I think that most lawyers, whether or not they chose to pursue opportunities at large law firms, always recognized the economic realities of practice.

But much of the mystique surrounding those firms and their partners has dissipated, largely due to the *American Lawyer* magazine, which was founded in 1979 by Steven Brill. Long before some associates began to blog anonymously about the dynamics of the firms they worked at, Brill's magazine focused on, and sometimes criticized, the financial aspects of large firms' operations.

Most significantly, in 1985, the magazine began to publish an annual list of the 50 highest-grossing law firms. In 1987, it expanded the list to 100 firms; and in 1999, it added a separate list of the next hundred firms.

Some readers have questioned the reliability and sourcing of the non-public information from which the rankings of the "AmLaw 50," "AmLaw 100" and "AmLaw 200" have been calculated. However, these lists—and particularly their estimations of "profit per partner" at each firm—have been widely credited with (and blamed for) increasing the mobility of individual partners, groups of partners, and sometimes entire practice groups (including associates and, possibly, support staff) to firms that they perceived would compensate them more appropriately.

This trend and others in the market for legal services, and in the economy in general, accelerated the transition by most major law firms from their traditional practice of "lockstep compensation," in which partners at the same level of seniority had been awarded the same proportion of their firms' profits, to so-called "eat what you kill" policies, in which a partner's compensation depends largely on her personal "rainmaking" (client- and assignment-generation) and billable-hour total.

In addition, some of the new systems replaced partners' expectations of effective lifetime tenure with the threat that those who could not continually satisfy the new metrics of productivity and profitability would have their shares of partnership profits reduced or even eliminated (in a process known as "de-equitization"), and that partners might even be expelled from the firm.

These developments have surely had dramatic and far-reaching effects on lawyers' loyalty to their firms and on the culture of large law firms individually and as a group.

In their defense, firms could well argue that retaining lockstep compensation would cause them to lose their most valuable partners and most promising associates to higher-paying competitors; that such departures could ultimately threaten the firms' very survival; and that, for years, every serious applicant for a position was or should have been well aware of the firms' general expectations.

Near the beginning of this trend, though, one partner sued his firm after a group of its partners changed its partnership agreement, arguing that they had effectively and unfairly expelled him. See *Beasley v. Cadwalader, Wickersham & Taft*, 1996 WL 449247 (Fla. Cir. Ct.) and 1996 WL 438777 (Fla. Cir. Ct) and Paul Barrett's front-page *Wall Street Journal* article, *Putsch and Shove* (August 17, 1998).

In agreeing with the plaintiff, the court disapprovingly quoted the following deposition testimony of a co-chair of the firm: "[L]ife is not made up of love, it is made up of fear and greed and money—how much you get paid[,] in large measure."

In the mid-2000s, a veteran partner at a large firm quietly told me, in what I took to be a reference to law firm partners generally, "If you're not an economic animal, they will eat you up."

- From a potential associate's perspective, one of the most interesting and entertaining (though now dated) books about big law firms was written by Cameron Stracher, who was in my law school class and first-year section. *Double Billing: A Young Lawyer's Tale of Greed, Sex, Lies, and the Pursuit of a Swivel Chair* (1998) features a law firm and characters described in an introductory note as "composites based on my experiences at several firms and on interviews I conducted with young associates," and cases presented "not. . . as literal fact, but rather as archetypes of the litigations in which I was involved." Spoiler alert: Although very well compensated, the author finds himself increasingly unfulfilled in this professional environment.

- Lincoln Caplan, *Skadden: Power, Money, and the Rise of a Legal Empire* (1993). A detailed profile of the history and culture of the legal powerhouse, and of the firm's role in and reaction to the rise in corporate mergers and acquisitions. Includes a discussion of the firm's process for selecting new partners. Chock-full of valuable lessons, great quotations, and revealing anecdotes.

- Kim Isaac Eisler, *Shark Tank: Greed, Politics, and the Collapse of Finley Kumble, One of America's Largest Law Firms* (1990). Eisler's colorful chronicle of the rapid rise and swift decline of this firm highlights issues of law firm culture, legal ethics, collegiality, and professionalism in general.

- Steven Kumble & Kevin J. Lahart, *Conduct Unbecoming: The Rise and Fall of Finley, Kumble* (1990). Kumble's own account of Finley, Kumble's history and his role in and reflections on it. Perhaps best read after Eisler's book, which does not present Kumble in an entirely flattering light.

- Ellen Joan Pollock, *Turks and Brahmins: Upheaval at Milbank, Tweed* (1990). A fascinating account of the history and internal repercussions of the firm's unexpectedly aggressive departure in the mid-1980s from the traditional lockstep compensation system in order to reward its rainmakers.

- Marc Galanter & Thomas Palay, *Tournament of Lawyers: The Transformation of the Big Law Firm* (1991). A detailed examination of the "promotion-to-partner tournament" among senior associates at large law firms, with a concluding warning of perceptions that such firms had "sacrificed client interests to market considerations" and "abandoned the[ir] collegiality and self-governance."

For a larger historical perspective, you might be interested in:

- Erwin O. Smigel, *The Wall Street Lawyer: Professional Organization Man?* (1964). A sociologist's report on his research, including interviews with 118 lawyers across 18 large law firms in New York City, and 44 lawyers across four large law firms from other geographical areas, on the conformity, creativity, and professional independence of lawyers in such firms.

  For purposes of his study, Smigel defined a large law firm as "one composed of fifty or more attorneys"; at that time, the largest firm in the city was Shearman & Sterling, with 125 lawyers. By comparison, *Tournament of Lawyers*, above, observed that "In 1968 the largest firm in the United States had 169 lawyers [and i]n 1988, the largest firm had 962 lawyers." And in June 2022, Law360 identified the largest United States-based law firm as Baker McKenzie, with 4,795 lawyers worldwide.

Chapter 30
Eight Virtues of Judicial Clerkships

You should consider applying for a judicial clerkship, especially in the geographic region in which you'd like to work.

What convinced me to apply were the unanimously positive stories that I heard from former clerks for a variety of courts. My clerkship, with Justice Daniel J. O'Hern of the Supreme Court of New Jersey, was one of the very best professional experiences that I've had.

A clerkship can be an extraordinary opportunity for several reasons.

First, and most generally, working for a judge will not only help you improve your legal writing skills but will also give you a chance to evaluate and learn from the legal writing and oral arguments of experienced practitioners, to see how they're received by the court, and to observe how the court and its administration operate.

Second, clerking for a specialized court like the Delaware Court of Chancery, or any bankruptcy court, will give you valuable experience in that subject area, whether or not you intend to practice in the geographic area of the court.

Third, while making the transition from academia to practice (although in recent years some clerks have already worked for several years at law firms or elsewhere), you'll be effectively working for only one person, instead of juggling assignments from several people.

Fourth, in the best of clerkships, I think the clerk feels like part of the judge's professional circle in some ways, and gains a mentor.

Fifth, a clerk's "backstage" perspective, while giving her a special vantage point from which to appreciate the intellects and personalities of judges, also makes judges somewhat more approachable and less intimidating to her on an emotional level. Watching, during my clerkship, an impressive oral argument to the Court by one of its former clerks, I suspected that at least part of his apparent ease was informed by his own experience as a clerk.

Sixth, you might learn many new lessons from the media reports on decisions that you've been involved with. How accurate are their initial summaries? How well do subsequent analyses and discussions reflect the subtleties of the decision and its implications?

Seventh, many potential employers recognize that, however good their own internal training programs are, you have a valuable experience and perspective, just as if you'd worked for a state or federal agency, that a law firm can't expect to replicate in-house.

Eighth, depending on the court for which you clerk, you might learn about a whole new level of collegiality and professionalism. As I wrote in my review on Amazon of Justice O'Hern's posthumously published profile of his fellow Justices and their work, *What Makes a Court Supreme: The Wilentz Court from Within* (2020), the book portrayed the members of the New Jersey Supreme Court during the 1985-1994 tenure of Chief Justice Robert N. Wilentz as a sort of judicial family.

However, there's a dimension of clerkships that isn't much talked about, a combination of intensity and isolation.

A clerkship will probably put you in a much smaller professional environment than you'd find in a law firm or in many other organizations. You'll be able to discuss the work, however compelling and fulfilling you might find it, only with the judge, any co-clerks, and any administrative assistants.

Also, for the term of the clerkship, you might have to move to an area that you don't plan to live in, or even near, after the clerkship ends.

For this reason, clerkship interviews, even more than law firm interviews, can involve the potential employer's and employee's getting a sense of each other as people and of whether they'll be comfortable working in close quarters with each other for a year or more. By contrast, in a law firm's interview, the hiring partner(s) and practice group leader(s) won't necessarily be the (only) people working with you; and in a law firm, you might be able to transfer to (or be transferred to) another group if some type of conflict or concern arises.

Although you might decide not to apply for clerkships with particular judges with whose published opinions you disagree, don't assume that such a judge will automatically exclude from consideration an applicant whose views and perspective differ from her own. Some judges even reportedly welcome divergent views in their chambers.

Yet it's possible that potential employers, colleagues, and friends might themselves assume that you share at least some of the views of the judge for whom you clerked; and because confidentiality restrictions remain even after the clerkship ends, you might not be able to clarify that issue for them as fully as you'd like.

Chapter 31
In Conclusion:
Of Keys, and Bees

Years ago, I saw on the front window of an American University shuttle bus a decal listing the Smith5Keys®[1] guidelines for safe driving. It struck me that, read figuratively rather than literally, those five principles summarize valuable reminders for law students.

First, *Aim High In Steering®*. For drivers, "A 15-second eye-lead time provides advanced warning and gives you an additional margin of safety."

Law students should similarly look "down the road," in selecting courses, considering potential employers and areas of practice, preparing for exams, and identifying timely paper topics. As hockey superstar Wayne Gretzky supposedly said, "I skate to where the puck is going to be, not where it has been."

Second, *Get The Big Picture®*. The Smith5Keys System reminds a driver to regularly check her side mirrors and to maintain enough distance to see ahead of the vehicles in front of hers.

Law students should avoid the "tunnel vision" of focusing exclusively on grades and exams. Instead, they should also pay attention to emerging trends in the law, economy, technology, and culture, and take into account how those might be, or already are, affecting the employment opportunities and prospects of new and recent graduates.

Third, a driver is advised to *Keep Your Eyes Moving®* every two seconds, to maintain alertness and peripheral vision and to avoid both distractions and apparently distracted drivers.

Law students should beware the temptations to multitask, particularly during classes; to overcommit to extracurricular activities; and to assume that they can easily catch up if they fall behind with their coursework.

---

[1] ®Registered. Smith System Driver Improvement Institute Inc., Arlington, TX, 76006. Used By Permission. See Smith System Driver Safety Training, *What Are the Smith5Keys?*, https://www.drivedifferent.com/smith5keys/ .

Fourth, a driver should *Leave Yourself An Out*®, by maintaining a "space cushion" on all sides of her vehicle.

Analogously, law students should incorporate extra time into their plans for finishing papers and studying for exams, to allow for last-minute problems or difficulties. Students can also design their selections of courses, writing topics, and job applications to preserve options in their employment opportunities.

Fifth, a driver in or around danger should *Make Sure They See You*® by using her vehicle's warning devices, instead of relying solely on eye contact with other drivers.

Law students are certainly well-advised to contact, as early as possible, their teachers with any substantive questions (including about how to study for an exam); to consult with the school's administrative offices if they feel the need for counseling or for some form of accommodation; and, in a different context, to increase their professional visibility by writing, blogging, making videos or presentations about, or otherwise notably engaging with timely legal topics.

One Final Note

For at least seven centuries, there has been a practice, among some of the Jewish communities of Eastern Europe and their descendants elsewhere, of giving to children, when they begin their religious education, a slate on which Hebrew letters have been written in honey. After licking the slate clean, the child might associate learning with sweetness and sustenance.

But that tradition also invites another analogy: between the honey—produced from the nectar collected from thousands of flowers by thousands of bees and slowly refined in beehives into a concentrated but easily assimilable source of nourishment—and the lessons, some clarified over many generations, that are carefully prepared and presented to students in their classes, coursebooks, and conversations.

Law schools might not always emphasize as much as they could the degree to which they are training law students not only to learn (and, as the cliché goes, to teach themselves), but also to teach—whether in their own articles, court pleadings, oral arguments, or presentations—their colleagues, clients, competitors, courts, and communities.

Appendix A
Thirteen Aspects of Preparing and Presenting "Actionable" Advice

Among the most frequently quoted lines of T.S. Eliot's poetry are those from 1934's *The Rock: A Pageant Play* in which he questioned whether we had lost wisdom in knowledge, and lost knowledge in information.

Those are certainly prime concerns of boards of directors.

For instance, the Corporate Governance Principles and Practices of Prudential Financial specify that, "The board should receive information important to understanding presentations, discussions and issues covered at each meeting, in writing and sufficiently in advance of the meeting to permit appropriate review. Longer and more complex documents should contain executive summaries. The focus of materials should be on analysis rather than data."

Perhaps the ultimate examples of the effective distillation and presentation of information are those discussed in *The President's Book of Secrets: The Untold Story of Intelligence Briefings to America's Presidents* (2016). Former CIA analyst David Priess provides an instructive chronicle of the origins, evolutions, and applications of the "President's Daily Brief" (PDB), which was prepared by the Agency beginning in late 1964 and which, since 2005, has been produced by the Office of the Director of National Intelligence (DNI).

That document summarizes for the Chief Executive "all relevant information from anywhere in the US government, presents an analytic message clearly and concisely, offers major alternative explanations, and highlights implications for US interests." In fact, "No major foreign policy decisions are made without it."

In light of the massive amount of sources and resources, including management and analyst time, involved in its preparation, the PDB has been described by a former Agency official as "the most expensive periodical in the world."

Priess, who personally briefed administration officials on the PDB's contents, interviewed "[e]ach living former president and vice president [and] almost every living former CIA director and deputy director for intelligence and the vast majority of other living former recipients of the book."

Their recollections and reflections offer at least fourteen practical lessons to lawyers, law students, and executives.

First, a counselor or advisor should present data and analysis that is "actionable," not in the lawyer's sense (as in, constituting grounds for a lawsuit) but in the intelligence community's meaning: capable of directly driving decisions by the principal, customer, or client.

One of the PDB briefers for President George W. Bush "challenged analysts to be able to compellingly finish the simple sentence: 'Mr. President, this piece is important because—.' If you can't fill in that answer, you don't have a piece. If you can answer it, you do—then you structure the piece to make that point clear, and quickly."

In his own book, *The HEAD Game* (2015), Philip Mudd recalls presenting a PDB item: "After I briefed the details of the threat, clearly and cleanly, I was satisfied. . . . Just as quickly as I'd spoken, though, a painful realization swept over me. I knew the briefing was wrong when [Bush] asked his first question. 'What do we do about this?' . . . I should have put the threat into context for him. . . ."

Second, brevity is crucial. The PDB is variously described as a "core six-to-ten page" document, supplemented by other material; containing "six to eight short analytic articles and additional items"; and usually including "two or three longer pieces, half a dozen intermediate-size ones, and then some quick little updates. I don't think it ever went more than ten pages long."

As Mudd put it, "The ugly secret for proud analysts is that. . . 90 percent of what they know (the data) might be useful at some other time, but it isn't today. A good analyst has to have the humility to accept that."

Similarly, Frank Watanabe's unclassified *How to Succeed in the [CIA's Directorate of Intelligence]: Fifteen Axioms for Intelligence Analysts* (1995; now available online)—which originally appeared in the Agency's periodical, *Studies in Intelligence*—advised, "The consumer does not care how much you know, just tell him what is important."

Third, the document should clearly distinguish facts from analysis. Robert Gates, CIA Director under President George H.W. Bush (and Secretary of Defense under Presidents George W. Bush and Barack Obama), instituted this policy in 1982, and one year later concluded to his analysts that "No other single change we have made has elicited as many favorable comments from consumers as this."

In fact, such an approach had briefly been adopted during President Richard Nixon's administration, in response to Attorney General John Mitchell's advice that "The President is a lawyer, . . . and a lawyer wants facts."

Fourth, say what you don't know. Colin Powell, former Secretary of State and Chairman of the Joint Chiefs of Staff, stated in his book, *It Worked for Me* (2012), "[O]ver time I developed for my intelligence staffs a set of four rules . . . I'm told they hang in offices around the intelligence world: Tell me what you know. Tell me what you don't know. Then tell me what you think. Always distinguish which from which."

Fifth, meeting these goals requires certain stylistic standards, as well as scrupulous editing. Watanabe reassured analysts, "Do not take the editing process too seriously. If editorial changes do not alter the meaning of what you are trying to say, accept them graciously[, but otherwise] do not be afraid to speak up and contest the changes."

Priess observes that a senior CIA officer "at one point even outlawed adverbs from the PDB, finding that analysts would then use the word 'because' more often and, as result, explain more clearly the reasons behind their judgments."

Sixth, formatting is also well worthy of attention. For each president, the CIA customized not just the PDB's content (including its balance of lengthy background analyses of issues with discussions of the families and personal interests of foreign leaders) but also its format (including whether to use footnotes and whether to leave large margins to allow for handwritten notes). In 2012, formatting issues literally took on new dimensions when Obama began receiving the PDF on an iPad.

However, the "First Customer" is not the famously indecisive protagonist of T.S. Eliot's *The Love Song of J. Alfred Prufrock* (1915). Watanabe warned, "Form is never more important than substance. . . [T]he consumer wants to know what the intelligence says, and he wants to know it when he needs to know it."

Seventh, visual elements can also be crucial components of the presentation. Under President Jimmy Carter, the CIA, "'trying to make it a little more attractive and easier to read,'" added "'a few more graphics. . . , charts and maps and photos and things that were a little more helpful.'" To aid the digitization of Obama's PDB, the Agency involved not only an "information technology expert," but also a "graphic designer."

In this context, counsel and others briefing clients might consider reviewing the classic works of Dr. Edward Tufte, such as *The Visual Display of Quantitative Information* (2d ed. 2001), *Seeing with Fresh Eyes* (2020), *Visual Explanations* (1997), and *Envisioning Information* (1990), as well as Stephen Few's *Show Me the Numbers: Designing Tables and Graphs to Enlighten* (2d ed. 2012).

For their own part, recipients of visual briefings could consult Alberto Cairo's examination of *How Charts Lie: Getting Smarter About Visual* Information (2019).

Eighth, in separating the text into paragraphs and bullet points, analysts and their editors should also take into account how recipients read, whether from paper or from a screen. These aspects of the PDB prepared for President Bill Clinton were carefully calibrated to reflect research on reading and retention of information.

Ninth, just like lawyers and executives, analysts should make special efforts to be aware of and to insulate themselves from possible cognitive traps and biases. An enlightening collection of "articles written during 1978-86 for internal use within the CIA Directorate of Intelligence," concerning "how people process information to make judgments on incomplete and ambiguous information," appears in *Psychology of Intelligence Analysis* (1999), by former CIA senior analyst Richards J. Heuer.

That book can well be read in conjunction with *Thinking, Fast and Slow* (2011), Nobel Prize-winning economist Daniel Kahneman's overview of his decades of research on these issues.

Tenth, as a former Deputy Director of Intelligence told Priess, "The conceptual breakthrough for me was that [the PDB] was an event, not a document."

That "event," and its process, both fostered and reflected many levels of relationships.

For example, the PDB has been shaped by decades of feedback and follow-up requests from presidents and their senior officials to CIA briefers, particularly after, upon taking office as Vice President, George H.W. Bush— himself a former Director of the CIA (January 1976 to January 1977)—requested daily personal briefings as he reviewed the document. That practice became standard for (or at least offered to) many, if not all, of the PDB's recipients.

Moreover, although the PDB seems to be the premier product among many that have been generated by elements of the intelligence community, it has been increasingly described as a joint effort of various agencies under the auspices of the DNI. As early as 1995, Watanabe advised analysts, "Know your [Intelligence] Community counterparts and talk to them. . . several times a month, not just when you need something," to foster "better collection, better products, less duplication, and less conflict over coordination."

Eleventh, it is not only corporations like Prudential that consider it "important that line and support unit managers make presentations to the board from time to time, to permit the board to have exposure to officers at various levels." As CIA Director under Carter, Admiral Stansfield Turner followed this practice in some PDB briefings.

In fact, under Director William Webster, to demonstrate the effectiveness of the CIA's disguises, the chief of that unit attended a PDB briefing session with her gender and ethnicity concealed, and during the meeting revealed her true appearance to the startled participants—although, Priess notes, President George H.W. Bush had caught on early. (In *Prufrock*, Eliot wrote of having time "[t]o prepare a face to meet the faces that you meet.")

Twelfth, both the client and the advisor should be mindful of the degree to which written reports can be protected from disclosure—whether by attorney-client privilege, or, in the specific context of the PDB (and of inquiries by the 9/11 Commission), executive privilege.

In 2002, Vice President Dick Cheney predicted to Fox News that making these closely held documents available to Congress "will have a chilling effect on the people who prepare the PDB. They'll spend more time worried about how the report's going to look on the front page of the *Washington Post* or on Fox News than they will making their best judgment and taking risk and giving us the best advice they can, in terms of what they think's going on."

(About thirteen years later, the CIA declassified and publicly released some PDBs prepared for President Lyndon Johnson, and similar documents from the Kennedy administration; in 2016, the Agency released some PDBs from the Nixon and Ford administrations.)

Thirteenth, and perhaps most important, is maintaining both the actual, and the perceived, independence of analysts and advisors.

Most of Watanabe's fifteen axioms urge the analyst to assertively prepare and promote her own assessments (including: "Believe in your own professional judgments"; "Be aggressive, and do not fear being wrong"; "When everyone agrees on an issue, something probably is wrong"; and, "Being an intelligence analyst is not a popularity contest").

Priess portrays the authors, editors, and personal presenters of the PDB as objective and nonpartisan walkers between worlds, bridging the realms of tradecraft and statecraft, catalyzing a dynamic interplay that at its best informs and enhances both.

Such is also, surely, the role played by many lawyers—for instance, as intermediaries among the developers of, users of, and investors in such emerging technologies as blockchain and cryptocurrency.

Appendix B
Enhancing the Decision-Making Process

In 1946, the beginning of Dr. Benjamin Spock's *The Common Sense Book of Baby and Child Care* advised parents to "TRUST YOURSELF. You know more than you think you do."

Although the latest edition of the best-seller retains this reassurance, which has been echoed by a number of authors (such as Malcolm Gladwell, *Blink: The Power of Thinking Without Thinking* (2005); and Gerd Gigerenzer, *Gut Feelings: The Intelligence of the Unconscious* (2007)), some of its newer companions on the nonfiction shelves warn that one's common sense, intuition, and self-confidence can be dangerously misleading.

Indeed, years after concepts of "behavioral economics" and "neuroeconomics" were recognized in law review articles, popularized summaries of decades of research in cognitive psychology and behavioral economics emphasize repeatedly how far removed most people are from another iconic Spock—the relentlessly logical science officer of *Star Trek*—by illuminating the blind spots (in technical terms, the "bounded rationality") that can betray even the most (subjectively) reasonable decision makers.

These books detail a disturbing variety of ways in which even people who embrace the rational rigors of decision theory, game theory, and systems analysis might naturally misjudge—or could easily be led to misjudge—the risks, rewards, and ramifications of their choices. As the title of The Main Ingredient's 1972 hit song both warns and reassures, *Everybody Plays the Fool* sometimes.

As corporate crises multiply locally, nationally, and internationally, directors and officers should be among the first in line for these mass-market, minimal-math mental manuals. After all, an executive's essential function is to make decisions, often under time and emotional pressure and with imprecise and incomplete information. Her fiduciary duties of care and loyalty thus demand that she understand and minimize the ways in which her own mental tools and techniques might be flawed or compromised.

Corporations require that employees who operate critical, sophisticated, and/or hazardous equipment be appropriately trained. They should similarly advise directors and officers to review the recently accessible lessons on optimizing the decision-making process. (Similarly, although most people usually leave their breathing to instinct alone, numerous classes, books, and videos offer simple techniques that purportedly enhance both the efficiency and effectiveness of the breathing process, and supposedly confer such other benefits as relaxation and increased resistance to stress.)

Such a cognitive curriculum would also help to immunize executives against aggressive attempts by their competitors, creditors, and customers to exploit the dozens of vulnerabilities identified by these works. Just being aware of those strategies—like being aware of the "good-cop, bad-cop" interrogation pattern, or of the deployment of extended silences (in the hope that the other person will feel pressured to start talking)—might automatically make someone more resistant to, if not entirely immune from, their effects.

On a more advanced, but ethically more questionable, level, executives aware of common cognitive vulnerabilities might only pretend to be succumbing to them—just as poker players study how to read body language, or "tells," not only to learn more about the strength of other players' poker hands, but also to understand how to mask their own inadvertent signals and even how to deliberately send the "wrong" signals.

In the same way that many lawyers prepare their clients to avoid psychological tricks and traps when being deposed or cross-examined, they should encourage executives to read (and might even summarize for them) some of the reporting on cognitive countermeasures. Of course, counsel could also apply this information to enhance their own adversarial and cooperative efforts, as well as the ways in which they offer recommendations to clients.

In addition, lawyers could take these issues into account in helping boards (perhaps with the assistance of experts to develop and implement strategies, ranging from specific plans and procedures to more fluid guidelines and lists of considerations, for resolving complex and crisis situations).

In the 1973 movie, *Magnum Force*, Clint Eastwood's Inspector "Dirty Harry" Callahan famously observed that "a man's got to know his limitations." Today, a surprising number of those foibles and fallibilities are wrapped up both literally and figuratively in bookstores across the country. Executives and their counsel can certainly afford to learn about them. Can they truly afford not to?

Below is a catalog of some of the patterns of pitfalls identified by behavioral economics researchers and commentators.

Related to Self-Centeredness

Affect Heuristic. Optimism in assessing an option that the decision maker likes and pessimism in assessing an option that she dislikes.

Cognitive Dissonance (also known as *Confirmation Bias*). Dismissing information or arguments that contradict a theory or conclusion that one has previously adopted. (*Cf. Motivated Reasoning*, the tendency to analyze more carefully and critically the ideas, theories, or analyses that contradict one's own.)

False Consensus Effect. Believing that one's own views and preferences are widely shared.

Unrealistic Optimism/Self-Confidence. Overestimating one's ability, and/or underestimating the time necessary, to overcome a challenge.

Confusing Confidence with Correctness. Assuming that one's confidence in a decision reflects the correctness of that decision.

Egocentric Bias. Overestimating one's own contribution to a problem and/or its solution.

IKEA Effect. Attaching an inordinately high value to items (such as pieces of furniture) that one has created (or even merely assembled) oneself.

Planning Fallacy. Focusing on the details of the immediate situation, without taking into account statistical or other information or perspectives on similar situations. May be linked to the *"Law of Small Numbers"*: Unjustifiably relying on small samples of a population to determine probabilities and proportions for the entire population

Plan Continuation Bias. Failing to reassess goals in light of new information.

Behavioral Confirmation Effect (also known as *the Pygmalion Effect*). Interacting with other individuals according to one's expectations or preconceptions of them, often leading to their (conscious or subconscious) conformity with those expectations or preconceptions.

Related to Overreliance on the Familiar

Tendencies Concerning Credibility of Information

Validity Effect (also known as *the Illusion of Truth Effect*). An unjustified sense that information is true, merely because one has encountered that information before. Linked to the *Common Knowledge Effect*: The tendency of members of a group to be more influenced by information that they had all been aware of than by information introduced to the group during the decision-making process.

Tendencies Concerning Evaluation of Prices or Positions

Anchoring. Inappropriately beginning a decision or analysis by focusing on a certain number or position, without independently assessing its own validity.

For instance, people furnished an initial numerical cue ("Do you think that the population of Manhattan is more, or less, than 17 million?") may tend to begin analyzing from that number (when subsequently asked, "How many people live in Manhattan?")—a boon to negotiators making opening offers, solicitors for donations ("Would you pay $10 for . . .?"), and salespeople setting prices (or imposing such limits as "12 cans per person").

Priming. A method of influencing decision makers by exposing them to information (even in a different context) before asking them to make a decision.

For example, college students in a "priming effect" experiment walked significantly more slowly after reading such words as "Florida" or "forgetful," apparently because they subconsciously associated such words with old age. In another test, people instructed to shake their heads from side to side were more likely to disagree with a message that they heard, while those told to nod were more likely to agree with it.

Status Quo Bias. Reflexive opposition to change.

Normalcy Bias. Denial of warning signs of danger or disaster.

Tendencies Concerning Assessment of Probability

Availability Bias. Focusing inappropriately on more recent occurrences.

Awareness Effect (also known as *Ready Recall Effect, Recency Effect, Vividness Effect*, or *Saliency Bias*). Overconcern with certain risks only because one has more awareness and/or readily available information about them. (Might also be called "misapprehension.")

Denominator Neglect. The tendency to be drawn to options whose vivid imagery (winning by blindly picking 1 of the 8 red balls contained in an urn of 100 balls, as opposed to selecting from an urn that contained 1 red ball among 10 balls) masks the lower probability (8% vs. 10%) of its success.

Hindsight Bias. Assessing, after an event has occurred, that it had been more likely to occur (and that it would have been easier to predict) than one would have estimated before its occurrence.

Black Swan Effect. Failure to envision or take into account the possibility of low probability but extremely disruptive events, and retrospectively rationalizing such failure.

Confusing Correlation with Causation (sometimes referred to as the fallacy of *post hoc, ergo propter hoc*—Latin for, "after this, therefore because of this").

Attributing Causality to Events Connected Largely by Chance/Luck.

Believing the "Law of Small Numbers." Drawing conclusions (such as that a roulette player is on a "lucky streak") based on a relatively small but statistically unusual sample and ignoring the tendency of "regression to the mean," i.e., for a larger sample of results (gathered from a larger population and/or over a longer time) to approach more closely the results predicted by mathematics.

Illusion of Control. Overestimating the degree to which one's skill influenced, or can influence, events.

Conjunctive Fallacy. Mistakenly concluding that a compound statement (for instance, "Jane is a college professor and wears glasses.") is more likely to be true than a single statement ("Jane is a college professor."). (Even though college professors may be more likely to wear glasses than other people are, logically the compound statement must be less likely to be true than the single statement.)

Tendencies Concerning Assessment of Utility/Value

Endowment Effect. Overvaluing an item one already owns, and charging a higher price to sell it than one would pay to buy it.

(Failure to Anticipate) Hedonic Adaptation. Not recognizing that the appeal of something currently attractive and/or novel may decrease over time.

Projection Bias (also known as Impact Bias). Predicting erroneously the value that one would attach to a possible future situation, especially by not considering that one's values, tastes, and preferences might change over time.

Social Comparison. Defining success by comparison to the status or situations of others, rather than in subjective or absolute terms.

Tendencies Concerning Avoidance of Risk

Certainty Effect. Preferring an opportunity for a certain gain, even if of a lower value, than the chance of obtaining a higher amount (for example, preferring a promise to be paid a certain $20 tomorrow to an even chance of receiving either $60 or $0 tomorrow).

Loss Aversion. Inappropriately large resistance to actual or prospective loss. (Related to *Sunk Costs*, the tendency to "throw good money after bad" instead of terminating a bad investment or course of action and recognizing, but limiting, one's losses from it.)

Tendencies Concerning Misevaluation of Information and Choices

Framing Effect. Perceiving an option as more attractive simply because the presenter emphasizes its positive aspect ("Seventy percent of patients suffer no significant side effects from this procedure") rather than its negative aspect ("Thirty percent of patients suffer significant side effects").

Halo Effect. Judging a person, thing, or company positively simply because one aspect of it appears to be attractive.

Choice Overload. Preferring a manageable number of options to a significantly larger number of options. See Sheena Iyengar, *The Art of Choosing* (2010).

Primacy Effect. Being overly influenced by the first elements of information presented during the decision-making process.

Recency Effect. Being overly influenced by the last elements of information presented during the decision-making process.

Compromise Effect. Avoiding one or more apparently extreme choices in favor of an intermediate option. (Related to the *Decoy Effect*, in which the deliberate inclusion of an inferior option enhances the decision maker's appreciation of the other choices.)

"What You See Is All There Is" Bias. Jumping to conclusions by basing results on limited data without taking into account its quantity and/or quality.

Preventive Procedures, Policies, and Protocols

Daniel Kahneman himself, at the conclusion of his book's extensive survey of cognitive traps, asked,

> How can we improve judgments and decisions, both our own and those of the institutions that we serve and that serve us? The short answer is that little can be achieved without a considerable investment of effort. . . . Except for some effects that I attribute mostly to age, my intuitive thinking is just as prone to overconfidence, extreme predictions, and the planning fallacy as it was before I made a study of these issues. I have improved only in my ability to recognize situations in which errors are likely. . . .
>
> Organizations are better than individuals when it comes to avoiding errors, because they naturally think more slowly and have the power to impose orderly procedures. Organizations can institute and enforce the application of useful checklists, as well as more elaborate exercises.

Types of procedures suggested by Kahneman and others are identified below. What are executives' and counsel's role in suggesting, implementing, or perhaps opposing the use of, these techniques?

Before Making the Decision

- Clarifying the company's assumptions, opportunities, and vulnerabilities, preferably in written reports.
- "[C]ollecting close call reports and measuring things that go wrong," then reviewing such incidents "to understand and address the root causes," sharing this information inside the company (and maybe the industry), and testing solutions to be sure they work. See Chris Clearfield & Andras Tilksik, *Meltdown: Why Our Systems Fail and What We Can Do About It* (2018).

  One practice, commonly associated with Toyota, involves investigating the source of a problem by asking "Why?" not once but five times (that is, demanding a further level of analysis four times, until the "root cause" is identified). See Jeffrey K. Liker, *The Toyota Way: 14 Management Principles from the World's Greatest Manufacturer* (2004).
- Scenario planning, that is, anticipating and preparing for emerging situations by identifying the information, participants, and trends that would be critical to the successful resolution of potential situation and clarifying their relationships and potential interactions. See Thomas J. Chermack, *Using Scenarios* (2022); Bill Ralston & Ian Wilson, *The Scenario-Planning Handbook* (2006); Peter Schwartz, *The Art of the Long View* (1991) and *Learnings from the Long View* (2011); and Kees van der Heijden, *Scenarios* (1991).

- Assessment of a company's physical and/or digital vulnerabilities by internal or outside experts, sometimes referred to as "red teams," "red cells," "tiger teams," "white hat hackers," "gray hat hackers," or "ethical hackers." See Micah Zenko, *Red Team: How to Succeed by Thinking Like the Enemy* (2015); Allen Harper et al., *Gray Hat Hacking: The Ethical Hacker's Handbook* (6th ed. 2022).
- "Premortems," in which the participants assume that the proposed course of action was taken and, at a specified future time, turns out to have been a grave mistake; they attempt to identify what could have gone wrong, and why.
- Clarifying elements of the decision's substance and process, including:
    - The exact question to be decided.
    - The nature (numerically, if possible) of potential successful and unsuccessful outcomes.
    - The time available to reach a decision, whether that time can be extended, and the default situation if no decision is reached.
    - What information is available.
    - What information is not available and when (if ever) it will be available.
    - How much information should be analyzed before a decision must be made.
    - How reliable that information should be.
    - How the decision makers should insulate themselves—and their decision—from confusing and/or malign influences.
    - At what point(s), if any, a decision will be reexamined and possibly modified.
- Creating processes for decision making in fast-developing and/or crisis situations. See Donald Sull & Kathleen M. Eisenhardt, *Simple Rules: How to Thrive in a Complex World* (2015).
- Continually applying the mathematical technique of Bayesian analysis to adjust, in light of new information or results, the probabilities assigned to the validity of a hypothesis. See James V. Stone, *Bayes' Rule: A Tutorial Introduction to Bayesian Analysis* (2013); Share Bertsch McGrayne, *The Theory That Would Not Die* (2011).
- Evaluating the desirability of various outcomes under Kahneman's "prospect theory," which, according to his book, diverges from standard economic theory in:
    1. establishing a "neutral reference point" by which to assess good (better than the reference point) or bad (worse) outcomes;
    2. reflecting a "diminishing sensitivity"—that is, less than perfectly linear change in the utility—for gains (or losses) beyond this point, since "the subjective difference between $900 and $1,000 is much smaller than the difference between $100 and $200"; and

3. incorporating the principle of loss aversion: "When directly compared or weighted against each other, losses loom larger than gains."

- Reviewing the principles of probability and statistics, in particular those concerning the riskiness of basing conclusions on small samples of data.

During the Decision-Making Process

- Keeping a decision journal noting what decisions were made and why, for subsequent review. (However, counsel may advise against generating contemporaneous documents that could be used against the corporation and/or its executives in litigation.)
- Minimizing the effects of "groupthink" by requiring participants in the decision-making process to prepare their initial analyses independently, and by appointing or retaining "devil's advocates" to challenge emerging majority opinions.
- "Satisficing," by settling for a result or choice that is "good enough" and moving on, rather than continuing to search for better options.
- Using a "maximin" decision rule by selecting the option that would lead to the least-bad worst-choice outcome.

After Making the Decision

- Conducting "after-action reviews," both for bad outcomes and good ones, to enhance the decision-making process for future situations.

Avoiding "Gumption Traps"

Near the end of his best-selling 1974 novel, *Zen and the Art of Motorcycle Maintenance*, Robert Pirsig addressed the avoidance of "gumption traps" that drain one's enthusiasm for, and attunement with, the process of accomplishing something—in his extended example (and analogy), of tuning and repairing a motorcycle.

Warning that "[t]he field is enormous and only a beginning sketch can be attempted here," he recommended such practices as maintaining "a notebook in which I write down the order of disassembly and note anything unusual that might give trouble in reassembly later on"; keeping "newspapers opened out on the floor of the garage in which all the parts are laid left-to-right and top-to-bottom in the order in which you read a page," to aid in efficient and complete reassembly; becoming familiar with suppliers of parts; and, in some cases, machining one's own parts.

Pirsig also provided remedies for "internal gumption traps," such as "an inability to revalue what one sees because of commitment to previous values" ("slow down deliberately and go over ground that you've been over before"); ego ("fake the attitude of modesty anyway"); anxiety (read deeply on the subject and make to-do lists); boredom (turn routine tasks "into a kind of ritual"); and impatience ("best handled by allowing an indefinite time for the job, particularly new jobs that require unfamiliar techniques; by doubling the allotted time when circumstances force time planning; and by scaling down the scope of what you want to do").

Finally, he suggested that to overcome "psychomotor traps," workers use good-quality tools, and arrange for comfortable lighting, temperature, and props. ("A small stool on either side of the cycle will increase your patience greatly.")

In focusing on undistracted immersion in activity, Pirsig prefigured, in some ways, Mihaly Csikszentmihalyi's 1991 examination of *Flow: The Psychology of Optimal Experience*, and of attaining "Zen-like" states while off the zafu (meditation cushion).

Pirsig reflected, "What I'm trying to come up with on these gumption traps, I guess, is shortcuts to living right"—and, famously, concluded, "The real cycle you're working on is a cycle called yourself."

Appendix C Fourteen Suggestions for Ethical Counseling in Fluid Situations

Herman Melville's *Bartleby, The Scrivener: A Story of Wall-Street* (1856), a perennial element of Law & Literature courses, concerns a concatenation of confrontations between "one of those unambitious lawyers who . . . in the cool tranquility of a snug retreat, do a snug business among rich men's bonds and mortgages and title-deeds" and a newly hired copyist, portrayed as "pallidly neat, pitiably respectable, incurably forlorn!"

Bartleby—mysteriously, and infuriatingly—soon declines every work-related request by saying, "I would prefer not to." Despite the extensive accommodations (some, literal) made for him by his increasingly aggravated (and never named) but not unkind employer, the short story does not end happily for the scrivener.

More than a century and half later, every junior lawyer, whether or not she is familiar with Bartleby's tale, can well anticipate the professional perils of his passivity.

Yet, unlike Bartleby, who was asked only to hand-copy documents (and to help check the accuracy of those produced by his colleagues), a junior lawyer (Jane), whether outside or in-house counsel, might well find herself without sufficient facts, knowledge of the law, or the time necessary to obtain either before having to advise a client. (The military, and some business commentators, have referred to as "VUCA" situations those that are volatile, uncertain, complex, and ambiguous.)

For instance, a shareholder, officer, or director (Charles) could insist that Jane provide quick legal advice during a corporate crisis, even though crucial details might not be available, and/or could be quickly changing, and although the relevant legal issues might involve several different (and not always fully developed) areas of practice.

Then, the law firm partner, or company's general counsel, for whom Jane works (Paula), herself handling urgent matters, might instruct Jane to, "Give Charles the best answer you can, under the circumstances, but don't expose us to malpractice liability or to charges that we violated professional ethics rules."

The very first of the ABA's Model Rules of Professional Conduct (MRPC) provides that "A lawyer shall provide competent representation to a client. Competent representation requires the legal knowledge, skill, thoroughness and preparation reasonably necessary for the representation."

Comment 3 to MRPC Rule 1.1 clarifies that in "emergency" situations during which it would be "impractical" for a lawyer inexperienced in a certain field to consult a lawyer better versed in it, she may provide advice "reasonably necessary in the circumstances."

Strategies (not legal advice) for Jane in such a situation might include:

First, establish who the client is: Charles personally, or the corporation that he might serve as a director or officer?

Anticipating that personal and corporate interests might diverge, MRPC 1.13(f) provides that in such cases Jane should clarify to the company's "directors, officers, employees, members, shareholders or other constituents" the identity of her client: "a lawyer shall explain the identity of the client when the lawyer knows or reasonably should know that the organization's interests are adverse to those of the constituents with whom the lawyer is dealing."

In fact, under MRPC 1.13(b), if Charles' proposed course of action (or inaction) would violate the law and harm the corporate client, Jane should "refer the matter to higher authority in the organization," and perhaps ultimately to the board or to the independent directors.

Second, despite Charles' requests for assistance "as soon as possible," Jane should check for specific deadlines for answering him and/or for his making a decision or otherwise taking action based on legal advice. Does he have a "hard" deadline, or would an extension be possible?

Third, to prevent any subsequent confusion about the basis for or validity of the advice, Jane should document in an e-mail to Charles (and cc'd to Paula) the information that Charles provided and his demand for an accelerated response.

Fourth, Jane should briefly summarize for Charles by e-mail (along with the deeper analysis) at least the first principles of the relevant area of law (for instance, a director's fiduciary duties of care and loyalty) and the aspects of those principles that are most applicable to the current situation.

Fifth, in that e-mail Jane could summarize at least the most relevant options (including Charles' taking no immediate action) and their relative advantages, disadvantages, and risks; and recommend, from a legal point of view, one of those options.

Sixth, Jane might generally be wary of making—or of helping Charles, or the corporation that Charles serves as a director or officer, to make—a predominantly "business decision," as opposed to offering the client her legal advice or perspective on a business situation.

According to Comment 3 to MRPC 1.13 (and bearing in mind, as discussed above, the lawyer's duty to report illegal conduct), not only must a lawyer usually follow a corporate constituent's decisions, "even if their utility or prudence is doubtful," but any "[d]ecisions concerning policy and operations. . . . are not as such in the lawyer's province." However, MRPC 2.1 does allow a lawyer to direct the client's attention to "moral, economic, social and political factors, that may be relevant to the client's situation."

Seventh, Jane and Charles might consider adapting to this context a Navy SEAL's advice concerning emergency decision-making in "life-threatening situations":

> Come up with three—and only three—possible options or courses of action. Look at the pros and cons of each option. Honestly weigh factors like risk, your ability to accomplish each option, and whether your plan is realistic. . . Then, without debating and rethinking each of your options, make the call and choose the one your gut tells you is the best. . . [M]ost importantly, be confident in your decision and proceed.

Cade Courtley, *SEAL Survival Guide: A Navy Seal's Secrets to Surviving Any Disaster* 23 (2012).

Eighth, Jane should indicate in writing to Charles what information (possibly in priority order) would be most useful for him or one of his colleagues to supply to her (or for Jane to gather independently, if given the necessary time).

Ninth, Jane should propose to Charles a specific schedule (rather than simply "as soon as possible" or "if anything new happens") to receive updates from him (and/or one or more of his colleagues) or to provide him with an updated analysis. She should make sure that she and Charles have complete contact information for each other (such as telephone numbers, e-mail addresses and texting information, and links and passwords to video conferencing and cloud storage systems that that they can both use).

Tenth, for especially sensitive situations, Jane should consider offering Charles and his colleagues any special encryption or other cybersecurity protections that she (or her firm) can make available on short notice and that she knows how to use. (Comment 8 to MRPC 1.1 reminds lawyers that to maintain their professional competence they should "keep abreast of the benefits and risks associated with [the] technology" of legal practice.)

Eleventh, Jane should ask Charles if she has, or can get (in writing, if necessary) his authorization to contact, and to request information from, his colleagues or other third parties and whether he needs to indicate that permission to them in advance. If Charles cannot grant such access, who can, and when, and how?

Twelfth, Jane should clarify, preferably by e-mail, what Charles has given her the authority to do, especially without further consultation with or authorization from him, on behalf of the client (whether that is Charles personally, or the corporation he serves). She should also check with him how she can, if necessary, obtain additional authorization.

Thirteenth, Jane might ask for Paula's approval to involve other members of the law firm (or department) and/or outside counsel or other advisors.

Fourteenth, if Charles is not already familiar with them, Jane should provide him with the names and contact information of those colleagues or third parties, alert them to the situation, and let them know whom they might expect to be contacted by.

Appendix D
A Sample/Starter Checklist for Drafting/Editing/Proofreading

Formatting

Are words spelled correctly and consistently?

Are defined terms used and capitalized consistently?

Are provisions, subsections, sections, and exhibits/appendices numbered and/or alphabetized consistently and without skipping numbers or letters?

The Parties' Relationship and Intent

Define the parties.

Can each party assign its benefits and/or obligations under the agreement?

Specify the relationship of this agreement to previous and/or concurrent agreements between the parties and/or between any party and a third party.

The Transactional Item, Rights, or Service

Specify/define the item or rights to be conveyed or service to be rendered.

Specify the timing of its being conveyed or otherwise provided.

Are documentation, training, maintenance, and updates included?

Is either party required to meet a certain standard of performance (such as reasonable efforts, best efforts, or an industry standard)?

Consideration

Specify/define the consideration given or to be given.

Specify the timing of its being conveyed or otherwise provided.

Term and Termination

What is the term of the agreement?

Can either party terminate the agreement before that time, and if so, under what circumstances and by what process?

If a court invalidates any specific provision(s) of the agreement, will that result in the agreement's termination?

Do any obligations (e.g., confidentiality) survive the termination of the agreement?

Notice

Does any aspect of either party's performance depend on the party's receipt of notice from any party or from a third party?

If so, how is such notice to be given, and when will it be deemed to have been received? Is notice considered to be effective upon its receipt?

Permission

Will any party's permission be required for another party to perform its obligations or to receive any benefits? Must permission always be prior, or can it be granted retroactively?

If so, how are requests for such permission to be made? How (in writing?), and how soon after receiving a request, must a party communicate its response? Is a failure to respond to be considered a rejection of the request?

Can the party from whom permission is requested deny to give permission "in its sole discretion," or is such a denial "not to be unreasonably withheld"?

Confidentiality/Nondisclosure

Is either party obligated to keep confidential the existence of the agreement and/or any or all terms of the agreement?

Is either party obligated to keep confidential any aspect of the material furnished to it by another party under the agreement? If so, how is that material defined by the agreement? Is the material itself required to be labeled or otherwise marked or designated as confidential, and the recipient prohibited from removing such designations?

What measures is the recipient of confidential material required to take to protect it?

Does the recipient have a duty to return the confidential material? To destroy the confidential material? (If so, how could such destruction be verified by the other party?)

Warranties

Are any express and/or warranties being disclaimed?

If so, is this disclaimer conspicuous?

Indemnification

Is either party required to indemnify the other in any circumstance?

Remedies

Does a party's delay in enforcing against another party its rights under the agreement waive its ability to exercise those rights?

In what circumstances do the parties agree that injunctive relief will be an appropriate remedy?

Is any party required to pursue available remedies in a specific sequence? If so, which party, under what circumstances, and what sequence?

Will a party's pursuit of one remedy prevent it from simultaneously or subsequently pursuing another remedy?

Liability

Are there any circumstances under which a party's failure to perform any or all of its obligations under the agreement will be excused?

Is there any exclusion of consequential, incidental, special, and/or punitive damages?

Is there any limitation of a party's liability, or limitation of the remedies available to another party, in any circumstances?

Is there any provision for liquidated damages to be paid by one party?

Dispute Resolution

Under what circumstances, if any, will disputes arising between parties concerning the agreement be resolved by mediation? By arbitration? How will such mediator(s) or arbitrator(s) be selected?

What happens if mediation fails to resolve the parties' differences?

Will the arbitration bind the parties? If not, what courses of action are available to a party dissatisfied with the result of the arbitration?

Venue and Governing Law

Do the parties agree that any litigation between them concerning the agreement will be brought in a specific state and/or federal jurisdiction and consent to that/those court's (courts') personal jurisdiction over them?

Do the parties specify that the law of a specific jurisdiction (not necessarily the same jurisdiction as that in which any litigation will be brought) will govern their dispute?

Amendments

By what process, if any, can the original agreement (and subsequently amended versions of it) be (further) amended?

Must such amendments be in writing? Must they be signed?

Entire Agreement

Does this document represent the "entire agreement" of the parties?

Date

Include the date of the agreement.

Is that different from the "effective date" of the agreement?

Include the dates of the parties' signatures, if different from the date of the agreement.

Appendix E
Policies, Procedures, and Practices for Decision-Making by Voting

In considering, or helping to establish, procedures by which partners, shareholders, directors, or others can reach decisions binding on themselves as a group, law students might consider the following general framework:

First, what issues has the particular group been given the power—by state or federal law or regulation, or by documents such as a partnership agreement, articles of incorporation, or corporate bylaws—to resolve by voting?

Second, what is the process for calling and holding a vote? By what means are parties qualified to vote to be given notice of and information about an upcoming opportunity to vote, and how much advance notice and information about the matter at issue should be supplied to them? By what methods, if any, can a party object to the validity of a group decision on the grounds that the party did not receive timely notice and/or sufficient information? At what point does a party's failure to raise such an objection constitute its waiver of the ability to object?

Third, who is eligible to vote on a particular issue? For instance, only members of a certain partnership committee, members of a specific board of directors committee, or holders of a certain class of company's shares?

Fourth, how much of a voice does each eligible voter have? Are votes cast *per capita* (one person, one vote), as is usual for a board of directors, or by the party's interest in the company, as is more common with shareholders (for instance, a holder of sixty of a company's sole class of shares would have twenty times the voice of a holder of three of those shares)?

Fifth, if the vote is not a "yes-no" or other two-option decision but instead involves a selection or selections among three or more options (for instance, in shareholders' election of two directors from among a group of five candidates), can voters cumulate their votes—that is, multiply the number of their votes by the number of selections they are allowed to vote for, and then distribute that total unevenly among their selections? (For instance, a holder of three of a company's sole class of one hundred shares could, in the election scenario above, have six votes—that is, three votes multiplied by two candidates—to cast, whether all on one candidate, or divided evenly between two candidates (the same as in non-cumulative voting), or unevenly.)

Sixth, does a quorum—or minimum amount of participation—exist? If not, the vote is not binding. A quorum of a board of directors or of a committee of the board is generally a majority of the respective group's members—but because in the context of a shareholder vote a quorum is generally a majority of the votes able to be cast on a particular matter (whether those votes are in favor of or opposed to a proposal is irrelevant for quorum purposes, so long as they have been cast one way or the other), a holder of more than half of a company's single class of shares might be able to satisfy the quorum requirement simply by voting its own shares—or, alternatively, could stymie the requirement by not voting at all.

Seventh, assuming that the quorum requirement has been met, what proportion of the votes must be cast in favor of a "yes-no" proposal in order for the proposal to succeed? In many situations, the default answer is, a majority of the votes actually cast (rather than a majority of the total number of votes that could have been cast).

Eighth, do eligible voters have a duty to vote? Directors, like state or federal legislators, generally do (and can be criticized for not participating in a vote), but shareholders, like voters in a local, state, or national election, generally have no legal (as opposed to civic or moral) duty to vote.

Ninth, do eligible voters have a legal responsibility to carefully obtain and review relevant information (duty of care) and to consider the interests of the larger entity (such as the corporation) over their personal interests (duty of loyalty) before casting their votes? Both of those "fiduciary" duties apply to directors and legislators, the former of whom can be legally liable to the company if they breach either or both of them, but, again, generally do not apply to shareholders or to voters in political elections.

Tenth, is there a public record of whether and how each voter voted? The votes of individual directors are preserved in corporate minutes, which shareholders may have access to; the votes of legislators are a matter of public record; but, although the participation of an individual in political elections might be recorded, the specific content of her vote will generally not be linked to her name.

Eleventh, who has standing to challenge a vote on the grounds that the procedural and/or approval requirements were not satisfied? What is the procedure for making such a challenge—and for, if the challenge is denied, making an appeal? To whom would such an appeal be made? Who has the burden of proof?

Appendix F
Topics for Papers and Blogs

Among the law firms whose Web sites provide notable collections and combinations of blogs are: Baker Donelson, Blank Rome, Chamberlain Hrdlicka, Cooley, Cullen & Dykman, Davis Wright Tremaine, DLA Piper, Dorsey & Whitney, Dykema Gossett, Faegre Drinker Biddle, Epstein Becker, Foley Hoag, Fox Rothschild, Holland & Knight, Keating Muething & Klekamp, Kelley Drye & Warren, Obermayer Rebmann, Orrick, Porter Wright, Seyfarth Shaw, Sheppard Mullin, Snell & Wilmer, Squire Patton Boggs, Stoel Rives, and Troutman Sanders.

Below are listed some broad categories of legal topics, from any of which you might isolate (and perhaps combine) issues on which to base a paper or a blog.

Accounting techniques/practices and the law
Activist investors (including their representation on corporate boards)
Advertising, marketing, and branding
Alcoholic beverages
Alien Tort Statute (re: alleged human rights violations by corporations)
Americans with Disabilities Act (ADA) implications for the design of Web sites
Animal law
Arbitration requirements in corporate bylaws (attempting to prevent class actions)
Art law
Artificial intelligence
Attorney-client privilege (applications, exceptions, and limits)
Augmented reality
Automation and artificial intelligence
Automotive data systems (including "black boxes"), safety, and privacy
Automotive law (including autonomous vehicles)
Aviation

Bankruptcy courts' approval/rejection of counsel and trustee applications for fees (and for) bonuses

Bankruptcy jurisdiction strategies of debtors, including the recent "Texas Two-Step"

Behavioral economics (including cognitive pitfalls; see, e.g., the works of Daniel Kahneman)

Beta test licenses (including their terms and their risks for licensees)

"Big Data" (also known as "predictive analytics") for clients and for lawyers; ensuring that algorithms operate equitably

Bioethics

Biometrics and privacy

Blockchain (also known as distributed ledger technology)

Bloggers as journalists (especially for purposes of protecting confidentiality of sources)
(and, more generally, the application of laws to bloggers and blogs)

C-Suite members (such as: Chief Executive Officer, Chief Operating Officer, Chief Financial Officer, Chief Information Security Officer, Chief Compliance Officer, Chief Sustainability Officer, and Chief Legal Officer) and their respective roles, responsibilities, and potential personal liability

Cannabis

Cause-based marketing

Cloud computing

Combating money-laundering

Companies' obligations to notify customers of potential/actual breaches of their privacy

Comparative corporate governance (and whether foreign practices should be adopted in the U.S.)

Competitive intelligence (including legal and ethical restrictions on these techniques)

Conflict minerals (corporate compliance/disclosures concerning the use of)

Construction law

Consumer protection (online and offline)

"Content curation"/"digital curation"

Contract/license drafting issues

Corporate codes of conduct (for officers and other employees and for directors)

Corporate compliance

Corporate liability to, and compensation of, mass-tort plaintiffs

Corporate monitors (functions and operations)

Corporate responses (individually and collectively) to SEC disclosure requirements

Corporate (and individual executives') use of social media; "social media policies"

Corporate waivers of the right to file for bankruptcy or of the application of the automatic stay

Creation of official committees in a corporate bankruptcy reorganization (standards for)

Crisis management, by clients and their counsel

Crowdfunding

Crowdsourcing

Cryptocurrencies and their regulation

Cryptocurrency as an asset in bankruptcy reorganizations

Cybersecurity of (and cybersecurity insurance for) companies and their counsel

DAOs (Decentralized Autonomous Organizations)

"Data scraping" (including legal and technical prevention; application of law of trespass to)

Decision-making (executive, counsel, and/or judicial) models and methods

Deferred prosecution arrangements of executives

DeFi (decentralized finance) (related to blockchain)

Digital rights management (DRM)

Directors and officers (D&O) insurance coverage and exceptions (including advance payment of their legal fees)

Distressed debt (also known as "vulture") investing, and claims trading

Drones

E-discovery

Electrically powered cars and trucks

Electing corporate directors (incl. proxy access, "zombie directors," board diversity, "critical mass")

Electronic health records (EHR) and electronic medical records (EMR)

"Electronic self-help" methods for licensors of intellectual property

Employee benefit plans

"Empty voting" in shareholder voting situations

Entertainment law

ESG (Environmental, Social, and Governance) initiatives of corporations, including "green," "sustainability," and "supply chain" efforts

Ethical issues for counsel

Ethical issues for corporate executives

Executive compensation (including "say on pay," "equitable compensation," SERPS, parachutes, clawbacks)

Fair Debt Collection Practices Act (FDCPA)

"Fair use" of copyrighted intellectual property, and its limits

"False light" publicity suits (particularly for material posted online)

Fan fiction (intellectual property issues)

Fashion Law

"Fast fashion" and sustainability concerns

Fintech (financial technology) (related to blockchain)

5G broadband cellular service
Foreign Corrupt Practices Act (FCPA)
Generic Top-Level Domains (gTLDs)
"Good faith": meaning, dimensions, and implications (incl. in Uniform Commercial Code, corporate, and other contexts)
Governance of close corporations
Governance of colleges and universities
Governance of corporations that are in bankruptcy proceedings
Governance of corporations that are insolvent but not (yet) in bankruptcy proceedings
Governance of financial institutions
Governance of healthcare institutions
Governance of limited liability companies (LLCs)
Governance of nonprofit organizations
Governance of religious organizations
Governance of "social enterprises" (e.g., benefit corporations, L3C's, B corporations)
Governance of transnational corporations
Green [that is, "sustainable"] bonds
Greenwashing and similarly misleading practices and the lawyer's role in preventing them (also, the definition of, and standards and metrics for, "green")
Hacking (incl. "ethical hacking"; zero day exploits; red cell hacking; and "hacking back")
Health care providers and institutions, including nursing homes and hospice care
Hospitality law
Immigration law
Impact investing
Indemnification of directors' and officers' legal fees (especially before the conclusion of legal proceedings)
Insider trading
Institutional investors (roles, positions taken by, activism and alliances of; influences on and by)
Internal investigations of corporations
Internet companies' (e.g., Alphabet, Amazon, Meta, Netflix's) compliance with foreign laws
"Internet of Things"
Jurisdiction over Web site operators (theories; "active" vs. "passive" sites; other tests and factors)
Key Employee Retention Plans/Programs (KERPS) and their treatment by bankruptcy courts
Law firm (and individual lawyers') effective and ethical use of social media

Lawyers' ability to ethically access and use social media created by opposing parties/counsel

Lawyers' obligations to protect client data files and digital communications

Lead directors of corporations (role and responsibilities of)

License terms that restrict rights granted to (or not denied to) licensees by copyright law

Long-term care facilities

Maritime law

Metadata (incl. possible ethical duties to remove it—and, on documents received, not to view it)

Mobile payment systems

"Morals clauses" for celebrities, executives, and others

Moral rights (not recognized by U.S. law, but can equivalents be created by contract/license?)

Municipal bankruptcies

"Name, Likeness, and Image" Rights of Athletes

Nondisclosure and trade secret agreements, and their exceptions and limits

Oil and gas law

Online bullying (including effective legal, technological, and cultural responses)

Online defamation (including effective legal, technological, and cultural responses)

Online gaming (including Esports, poker, and videogames)

Online music (especially licensing and intellectual property issues)

Online privacy protection (including "do not track" proposals and technology)

Open source licenses; freeware; General Public License (GPL); "copyleft"; Creative Commons

Personal criminal liability of corporate executives

Personal privacy of corporate executives (incl. health issues, and "public figure" status)

Pharmaceuticals

Plagiarism (definitions, tolerance of; legal and social punishment of; compare to copyright infringement)

Political contributions (and disclosures of such expenditures) by corporations and executives

Products liability (including for medical devices and for pharmaceuticals)

Products liability claims and claimants, and their treatment in bankruptcy reorganizations

Proposals for the reform of Chapter 11 bankruptcy reorganization

Protecting children who use the Internet

Protecting older adults who use the Internet

Proxy advisors: their role and responsibilities (and regulation?)

Psychedelic drugs (and their legalization for certain purposes)
Revenge pornography (the laws concerning)
Review sites (such as Yelp) (including recourse for those objecting to reviews)
Risk management
Robotics
Search engines (including paid advertising, search engine optimization (SEO), use of metatags)
Shareholder proposals (including those for corporate disclosure of operational information)
Shrinkwrap, clickwrap, and browsewrap licenses (drafting, terms, and enforceability)
Social impact bonds
Social influencers
Socially responsible investing (SRI) funds and social impact funds
Source code escrow arrangements
Sports law
Spyware (incl. license terms, and legal and technological attempts to repel it)
Superhero characters and their "universes" as intellectual property
Telematics
Theories of civil liability for executives (e.g., responsible corporate officer doctrine)
3D Printing
Tobacco products, and vaping
Treatment of retiree/pension benefits in (municipal and/or corporate) bankruptcies
Veterans
Web3
Whether a director may—and should—publicly dissent from positions or processes of the board
Whether executives have a duty not to embarrass their firms by private and/or public behavior
Whether lawyers have a duty not to embarrass their firms/clients by private and/or public behavior
White collar criminal defense
Woonerfs and other traffic arrangements

Appendix G
Zen and the Art of Crisis Management

For one month during the summer of 2008, what became known as the Basin Complex Fire threatened to engulf the wilderness-surrounded monastery, Tassajara Zen Mountain Center ("Tassajara"), a central California coast component of, and at that time the generator of almost half of the operating expenses of, the San Francisco Zen Center (the "Center").

Colleen Morton Busch's engrossing *Fire Monks: Zen Mind Meets Wildfire at the Gates of Tassajara* (2011) examines in illuminating detail how the community's commitment to and concentration on meditative practices prepared it to respond to this emergency.

Of crucial concern were Tassajara's isolation—it could be reached by only one road, which might well be cut off by the fire—and the readiness of fire authorities to prohibit anyone who left from returning until the emergency had ended. There would thus be a temporal and physical "point of no return"—or, what Amazon's Jeff Bezos has famously characterized as a "one-way door" decision.

Busch's detailed account of the community's dynamics in confronting as "a field test for Zen practice" such a (figuratively and literally) elemental threat to its physical facilities—and to its spiritual, organizational, and financial stability—holds many lessons for directors, officers, and counsel of companies coping with crises.

Among them (without spoilers, as far as possible):

First, assess realistically the capacities of potential members of the crisis team and of its leadership group, especially if only a limited number can participate.

Summer guests were immediately evacuated; and law enforcement and firefighting authorities, who had originally declared that everyone should leave, ultimately told Tassajara's leaders that at most eight longer-term residents could remain. In an early sign of the community's independent approach, fourteen members stayed on (several other supporters would arrive later), and agreed that six would "function as a decision-making team." Nonetheless, by a relatively early point, "half of the senior staff had been evacuated."

Second, establish quickly each team member's role and relative authority in the decision-making process. Two residents left after becoming concerned that there was no clearly defined "trigger point" for the evacuation of the entire group. At a critical juncture, this very issue would divide: Tassajara's director, David Zimmerman; one of the Center's Abbots ("a position of both spiritual and organizational leadership"), who had arrived four days after the state had ordered all "nonessential" people to leave; the other Abbot, who telephoned Zimmerman a week later; and a resident who also captained a station of California's firefighting agency.

One of the four later "insisted that he made the right decision. . . with the information he had at the time." A second recalled, "We respected [that person's] decision. But we weren't fully persuaded by it." A third would tell Busch, "I could have done something there to better communicate." And the fourth—who had opposed creating the "trigger point," on the grounds that "We wanted to respond to events as they arose rather than draw a line in the sand"— would conclude in a post-crisis message to the community, "The decisions we make may not be the 'right' ones, but they are simply the best decisions we can make in the moment before us."

In such a fast-moving situation, who can make suggestions, recommendations, or requests to—or command, order, or overrule—whom? As matters progressed, and over the on-scene Abbot's objection, the Center's president, who had not had fire training, attempted to join the group at Tassajara. However, he and the treasurer were intercepted and turned away by a police officer who simply refused to discuss the issue with them. (A curious aspect of the book is the almost-complete absence of any reference to the Center's board of directors or other governance structures.)

Third, apply the community's values, perspective, and training to the situation. As Busch notes, Zen practice "teaches. . . not simply how to be quiet and still. . . but how to let that measure of equilibrium accompany you when you leave the [practice hall]."

Fourth, determine and refine as best you can not just goals but their respective priorities, the parameters of "success," and (since fire often reemerges after apparently having been extinguished) how to detect when the crisis has ended.

Fifth, know what the law is, and how it—and the prospect of personal liability—might affect participants' decision-making. Just as some firefighters see their *Ten Standard Fire Orders* (fdacs.gov/Forest-Wildfire/Wildland-Fire/Fire-Safety/Ten-Standard-Fire-Orders), which include, "Be alert. Keep calm. Think clearly. Act decisively," as "'ideally possible but practically unattainable,'" some of the residents were aware that, despite its name, California's "mandatory evacuation" order does not enable authorities to force residents to leave, and they had learned that one can in some circumstances legally ignite "backfires" on one's own property to protect it from more serious damage.

But the Tassajara group did not fully appreciate that a new awareness of potential liability had made incident commanders more cautious about putting their firefighters' lives at risk and about discussing decisions with outsiders.

And, although residents who chose to stay were asked by firefighters to provide not only emergency contact information but also the names of their dentists (for the possible identification of bodily remains), the leaders of Tassajara and the Center apparently did not require, or even ask, them to sign waivers absolving the institutions from liability for their deaths or for any injuries that they might sustain.

Sixth, consider carefully the commitments and commands of, and conflicts among, external authorities. Several times, Tassajara leaders' expectations of assistance were disappointed, and it was not always clear which of the official firefighting forces had jurisdiction and control.

Seventh, maintain both internal and external lines of communication. Firefighters as well as residents continuously monitored weather reports (and did their own fire spotting from various vantage points) as the fire grew larger and nearer. The core members of the Tassajara group stayed connected through walkie-talkies, into one of which the leader of the firefighters had programmed the frequencies that some of the firefighters would be using to speak with each other. From afar, some members operated a blog providing frequent updates on Tassajara and kept in touch with reporters, even as the Center's president tried to get help through its political connections.

Eighth, review the organization's experience in previous situations and keep records of the current circumstances and decisions. At the first indication of danger, Zimmerman consulted Tassajara's "fire log" from the Marble Cone Fire thirty-one years before; and he carefully typed up his own handwritten notes "to leave behind a thorough written record. . . like the ones he'd been reading." (The firefighters maintained their own official Key Decision Log.)

Ninth, prepare for recurring situations by stocking up on equipment and ensuring that members have appropriate training. Tassajara had amassed a supply of high-quality fire protection gear, and had constructed a special standpipe system to deliver strong flows of water for firefighting. However, only one of the key group of residents had "any current wilderness first-aid training."

Tenth, conduct practice drills, which might include a "'ready-for-anything crew' [to stand] by, [as] an extra set of hands, ears, and eyes."

Eleventh, maintain, to the degree possible, the organization's ordinary routines—in Tassajara's case, its regular meditative services.

Finally, be prepared for criticism, both from outsiders (that members had not helped neighbors cope with the fire) and from insiders (over the core group's ultimate decisions about complete evacuation).

Busch's sympathetic profiles of key participants (including a couple having problems in their relationship) and her chronicle of their often intense interactions are not without what some readers might call "woo-woo" moments. For instance, one of the Abbots told a reporter, as the deadly fire neared, "We're not really fighting the fire. We're meeting the fire, letting the fire come to us, [to] make friends with it, tame it as it reaches our boundaries."

He also professed "confidence in [spontaneously and intuitively perceptive] beginner's mind [and in] the willingness to remain completely present and not turn away from the unknown." However, one of the firefighting authorities advised a resident, "The difference between a professional firefighter and you is[,] I know what to be afraid of,"; and another firefighter had come increasingly to appreciate a senior colleague's professional motto, "When in doubt, chicken out."

The same Abbot characterized Zen practice as "very straightforward and direct. . . You take care of what is in front of you. You do what you can, and when you can't, well, ok, then you can't." Busch reports that, consistent with their training, residents protecting the monastery "just did the next thing and the next thing, continuously. They did what they could do and didn't dwell on what they couldn't."

But as Busch chronicles, for a number of individual residents protecting the monastery, and for the community, the decision to stay, and thereby to assume very serious risks, wasn't necessarily "straightforward and direct" at all.

In fact, though each member of the Tassajara community—and of the firefighting and law enforcement authorities involved—appears to have been acting entirely in good faith, people ended up disagreeing on critical issues. And more than one person at Tassajara would ultimately change his or her decision about whether to evacuate.

Whether or not they practice Zen meditation, corporate directors and their counsel might regularly reflect on the relevance to their own responsibilities of Tassajara-affiliated poet Jane Hirshfield's (almost-haiku) summary of Zen wisdom: "Everything changes. Everything is connected. Pay attention."

They might also consider Busch's observation that for the "Fire Monks" of Tassajara, "[a]s with Zen practice, the point wasn't to create some static state of permanent protection. The point was to be perfectly ready for whatever comes." Or, as Van Halen sang in *Jump* (1983), "You've got to roll with the punches and get to what's real."

Appendix H
Creative Career Suggestions for ESG and Corporate Law

Below are some (sometimes overlapping) categories of private firms and organizations that students interested in ESG and corporate law might consider when broadening the scope of their searches for employment.

The specific entities identified are included as examples, and no endorsement of their specific services, methods, positions, or policies should be inferred. They might not necessarily offer summer positions or positions immediately upon graduation.

Investigative Firms—offer assistance in: gathering and analyzing "competitive intelligence" information about the activities and operations of clients' competitors; "due diligence," in researching individuals, companies, and other elements of a client's proposed transactions; and compliance, ensuring that clients don't violate applicable regulations or statutes.

Kroll; K2Integrity; Fuld & Company; Stratfor; Investigative Group International; Arkin Group; Gryphon Strategies; AlixPartners

Crisis/Risk Management and Public Relations Firms—help clients communicate with the press and with shareholders, particularly in situations of apparent or suspected wrongdoing by the company and/or one or more of its executives.

Fairfax Group; Makovsky; Levick; Joele Frank; Ketchum; Protiviti; The Dilenschneider Group; The Toerrenzano Group

Claims Trading and "Distressed Debt" Investment Firms—acquire the legal claims held by other parties against a troubled company (for example, by buying some of the company's bonds from its bondholders) and become involved in the commercial resolution of the company's situation (before and/or during bankruptcy) to maximize their compensation for those claims. May also buy securities of the failing firms. Sometimes known as "vulture investors." For more information, see Hilary Rosenberg, *The Vulture Investors* (1992, revised 2000); and Sujeet Indap & Max Frumes, *The Caesars Palace Coup* (2021).

Monarch Alternative Capital; Alden Global Capital; Argo Partners; Marblegate Asset Management; Claims Recovery Group; Avenue Capital Group

"Turnaround" and Restructuring Consultants—advise financially troubled companies and might help them enter, and/or guide them through, the bankruptcy reorganization (Chapter 11) process.

AlixPartners; O'Keefe & Associates

Management Consultants—help companies formulate and implement business strategies. For critical accounts of their operating premises and services, see Walt Bogdanich & Michael Forsythe, When McKinsey Comes to Town (2022); Duff McDonald, *The Firm* (2013); Walter Kiechel, *The Lords of Strategy* (2010); Matthew Stewart, *The Management Myth* (2008); and James O'Shea & Charles Madigan, *Dangerous Company* (1997).

The Boston Consulting Group; Bain & Company; McKinsey & Company

(Firms that advise the management of law firms on expansion, compensation, market positioning, and other issues include Altman Weil, HBR Consulting, and the Zeughauser Group.)

Director and Officer ("D&O") Insurance Carriers—offer insurance (usually paid for by the corporation) to protect individual executives from personal liability for their actions (or inaction) in connection with the company's activities.

Aon; Chubb Group; Travelers

Compliance Trainers—provide corporate employees with information and guidance on observing the restrictions of relevant statutes and regulations; may help a company design and implement compliance processes.

Trace International; Deloitte & Touche (compliance group)

Executive Training and Education Groups—may include development and discussion of "best practices" for governance in a given profession or industry, or across professions and industries.

The Conference Board; Gartner; MetricStream; Forum for Corporate Directors

Executive Recruiters—help boards identify and approach candidates for officer positions.

Korn Ferry; Lucas Group; James Drury Partners; Heidrick & Struggles; McCormick Group; Pearson Partners International

Executive Compensation Consultants—provide boards and/or their compensation committees with information and advice on the appropriate amount and components (salary, bonuses, stock, stock options, perquisites) of compensation for officers.

Compensation Resources; Pearl Meyer; Compensia; FW Cook; Mercer; Semler Brossy; Aon; Exequity

Shareholder Communications, Proxy Solicitation, and/or Voting Tabulation Firms—distribute (and may help prepare) information and ballots provided to shareholders by the board; may tally shareholder votes and/or facilitate shareholder meetings.

Laurel Hill Advisory Group; Georgeson; AST Fund Solutions; Broadridge; Proxy Services Corporation; Egan-Jones Proxy Services; IVS Associates; Corporate Election Services

Proxy Advisors/Proxy Firms—advise shareholders (usually not personal "retail" shareholders but "institutional" shareholders (see below) like pension funds) on voting for or against governance proposals generated by the board or by other shareholders; might (proxy firms) themselves vote the shares on behalf of their shareholder clients.

Institutional Shareholder Services (ISS); Glass Lewis; Egan Jones

Credit Rating Agencies—evaluate and rate the riskiness of corporate bonds.

Moody's Investor Service; S&P Global Ratings; Fitch Ratings; Kroll Bond Rating Agency; Egan-Jones Rating Company

Governance, Sustainability, and/or ESG Rating Firms—assess, through proprietary methods, the environmental operations, social initiatives, and/or governance of individual corporations.

MSCI; Sustainalytics; FTSE Russell; S&P Global Ratings

ESG Consultants—assist companies in developing and implementing aspects of ESG programs.

Anthesis; Framework ESG; Trinity Consultants

Hedge Funds—investment funds that are relatively unregulated (as opposed to, for instance, mutual funds), that do not sell interests to the public in registered public offerings, and that generally count high-net-worth individuals and institutional investors among their investors. May make relatively short-term investments in companies. See Sebastian Mallaby, *More Money Than God* (2010).

Citadel Capital; Paulson & Company; D.E. Shaw Group; Caxton Associates

Private Equity Firms—generally operate by acquiring controlling blocks of shares of corporations and then taking them private. Often seen as requiring longer-term commitments from their own investors than do hedge funds. For a superlatively favorable account of their operations and internal dynamics, see Sachin Khajuria, *Two and Twenty* (2022).

Blackstone; The Carlyle Group; Kohlberg Kravis Roberts & Co.

Venture Capital Firms—purchasers of stock in newly founded or relatively young companies that are not yet publicly traded; often participate actively in the company's governance. See Sebastian Mallaby, *The Power Law* (2022).

Accel; Bain Capital; Benchmark; Greylock Partners

Counsel for Shareholders in Derivative Lawsuits and/or Class Actions—represent shareholders against corporations and/or their executives (for instance, in challenging merger transactions).

Bernstein Litowitz Berger & Grossman; Block & Leviton

Litigation Funding/Investment Firms—finance actions against corporations and/or their executives, in exchange for a proportion of any damages awarded to the plaintiffs.

Parabellum Capital; Blackrobe Capital Partners; Omni Bridgeway; Juridica Investments; Burford Capital

Institutional Investors.

TIAA (Teachers Insurance and Annuity Association-College Retirement Equities Fund); CalPERS (California Public Employees' Retirement System); CalSTRS (California State Teachers' Retirement System; Council of Institutional Investors; AFL-CIO (American Federation of Labor-Congress of Industrial Organizations)

Activist Investors—acquire significant amounts of shares and attempt to influence management's decisions, and might seek to seat their own candidates on the board.

Icahn Management; Elliott Management; Relational Investors; Third Point; Starboard Value; Pershing Square Capital Management; Trian Fund Management; MHR Fund Management; Jana Partners

Shareholder Activist, Corporate Watchdog, and ESG Advocacy Groups—monitor corporate activities and identify potential abuses.

As You Sow; Corporate Accountability International; Ceres; Climate Action 100+; Interfaith Center on Corporate Responsibility; US SIF: The Forum for Sustainable and Responsible Investment; The Global Impact Investing Network; Green America; Proxy Impact; Proxy Preview; SOC Investment Group

Impact Investing Funds—design their portfolios of holdings to support companies engaged in ESG initiatives.

Domini Social Investments; Calvert Impact Capital; Trillium Asset Management; Green Century Funds

Organizations that Certify, Advise, Support, and/or Fund "Social Enterprises"—businesses that are designed not only to make a profit but also to meet one or more ESG goals.

B Lab; Ashoka; Omidyar Network; New Profit Inc.; Schwab Foundation for Social Entrepreneurship; Social Enterprise Alliance

Organizations About Governance Issues.

Association of Corporate Counsel; Business Roundtable; Council of Institutional Investors; International Corporate Governance Network; National

Association of Corporate Directors (NACD); Society for Corporate Governance; National Investor Relations Institute

Organizations Concerned with Governance of Non-Profit Entities.

Hurwit & Associates; BoardSource

Organizations for Enhancing Board Diversity.

Alliance for Board Diversity; Athena Alliance; Boardlist; Boardroom Bound; Catalyst; DirectWomen; Ellevate; Executive Leadership Council; 50/50 Women on Boards; Hispanic Association on Corporate Responsibility; International Women's Forum; Interorganization Network (ION); New America Alliance; Next Gen Board Leaders; 30% Club; 30% Coalition; Women Corporate Directors; Women in the Boardroom; Women2Boards

Also note: Minority Corporate Counsel Association